Reading this book, I was reminded that our most healthy posture in life is receiving mentorship from those who have traveled ahead of us, while mentoring those who come along behind. In *Bigger Than Me*, I find Ward Brehm there—a recipient of tremendous experience and knowledge (the book is rightly dedicated to his mentors) and also a generous conduit of wisdom and hard-won insight. This book is more mentorship than memoir, beautifully so, and has the candor of a friend showing the way.

—*Sarah Groves, internationally known contemporary Christian singer, record producer, and author*

The most important things in life are not what we acquire or achieve but the fingerprints we leave behind on other people's lives. Ward Brehm leaves some great fingerprints in *Bigger Than Me*.

—*Cris Carter, member of the NFL Hall of Fame and sports analyst for* Fox Sports

Rather than just talking about a purpose-driven life, Ward Brehm has actually lived one. From his more than fifty trips to Sub-Saharan Africa working on creative solutions to extreme poverty to acting as an unofficial ambassador for Jesus in Washington, DC, Ward's life is a rarity in today's world: a life of faith based on relationships verses transactions. He can be trusted. In *Bigger Than Me*, Ward lays out much wisdom for every age.

—*Gov. David Beasley, executive director of World Food Program and former governor of South Carolina*

Ward Brehm has had a remarkable and inspiring journey. In *Bigger Than Me*, he graciously shares what he has learned along the way. Just as his faith and his work in Africa have transformed his life, reading his words can transform ours.

—*US Senator Amy Klobuchar*

Much like Ward before his transformative first trip to Africa, a trip he didn't even want to take, I didn't really want to read this book. I thought I already knew his story inside and out. However, after I began reading about his journey of faith, I was captivated, inspired, and motivated to continue reaffirming my faith on a daily basis.

—*US Senator John Boozman*

Ward opens his heart in this inspiring book and talks vulnerably about how he found his core significance by following Jesus. What great joy there is in realizing that life isn't about how much we can accomplish or how busy we can be but about loving God and our neighbors with everything He's given us. This book is a must read. You'll be encouraged and challenged by it.

—US Senator Jim Inhofe

I never get tired of stories about God taking someone on a 180-degree turn toward His purposes. That's Ward Brehm's tale in *Bigger Than Me*. A reformed "jerk" who learned to stop living for self and success, Ward found deep significance in following Jesus to care for the "least of these." There's nothing boring about where that path led him. As a believer who has been on a similar journey, I can confirm that living out God's will is the adventure of a lifetime!

—Rich Stearns, president of World Vision U.S.
and author of The Hole in Our Gospel

"Seek and ye shall find." Ward Brehm's inspiring book, *Bigger Than Me*, tells us not to listen for God's booming voice but to examine our life's journey and find His hand. Ward never preaches, but his examples of joy from giving of self certainly qualify him as a spiritual guide. He is a seeker who has found a great deal from which we can learn.

—Marilyn Nelson-Carlson,
chair of The Carlson Companies

When the "shoes" that Ward's book sews fit you, wear them. You will be better for having done so, even the uncomfortable ones.

—Greg Page, former CEO and chairman of Cargill Inc.

Bigger Than Me is really a travel book. In moving terms, it documents one man's faith journey—the twists and turns, the ups and downs, the unexpected adventures. With every step and with every adventure, Ward becomes a better man, and I found myself challenged to reflect on these most important lessons.

—Mark Green, administrator of USAID
and former US congressman

If you are blessed, truly blessed, someone will show up and completely change your perspective on life. Ward Brehm was that someone for me. One night, during a trip to Rwanda, Ward looked at me and said something simple yet transformative: "We spend the first half of our lives seeking prosperity, and if we're lucky, we spend the second half seeking purpose." Reading *Bigger Than Me*, you can't help but be inspired by the story of an everyman who broke loose from his comfortable surroundings and found his purpose in a continent far away.

—*Jack Leslie, chairman and CEO of Weber Shandwick*

Ward Brehm is the pastor to his pastor! If I put into one place all his words of comfort, wisdom, and challenge to me over the years, it would become this book, *Bigger Than Me*!

—*Rev. Dr. John F. Ross, senior minister,*
Wayzata Community Church

Bigger Than Me is a fascinating personal story based on authentic real-world experience and candor. It offers wisdom and inspiration for those seeking to live a purposeful life in a complex and perplexing world.

—*Ed Meese, US attorney general*
under President Ronald Reagan

Ward's sharing of his faith journey in *Bigger Than Me* challenges us to quit following dime-store maps and instead reorient our lives so we can discover and fulfill our God-given purpose.

—*Hon. Kathleen Blatz, former chief justice,*
Minnesota Supreme Court

Bigger Than Me is a refreshing book about faith that looks at the perplexing whys in life but doesn't preach. It's an easy read, yet I often stopped to ponder key answers. This book will help you remember and see purpose in the big and small, happy or tough events in your own life.

—*US Senator Mike Enzi*

Ward's life is a remarkable example of personal growth and transformation, and through it he has touched many lives. *Bigger Than Me* is a wonderful story about finding God and walking with Him.

—*Tony Hall, former US congressman and US ambassador*
to the United Nations agencies on hunger
and three-time Nobel Peace Prize nominee

Bigger Than Me is the moving testimony of an American "big dog" who thought he had life all figured out—until, that is, he met some people in Africa who had nothing and had life figured out a lot better than he did.

—*Joe Richie, founder of Chicago Research and Trading (CRT)*
and Fox River Partners

I saw myself in Ward's story, as I think many people will—the death of a parent, a crisis of personal meaning and faith, a desire to serve, the struggles and triumphs of family, and ultimately one's own life journey. But above all, Ward's story is an unwavering, optimistic belief in the inherent good of people in the world and their need to connect with you as an equal—to see and be seen. Both big and small, human and global, intimate and universal, he tells a story that is in equal parts personal and profound.

—*Paul Bennett, chief creative officer of IDEO*

Planet Earth offers a whole lot, but none of it compares with a closer walk with Jesus. My friend Ward Brehm knows both. He also knows that the pursuit of faith can be blocked by our own baggage and worldly attractions. In *Bigger Than Me*, he knocks down the barriers a chapter at a time.

—*Jay Bennett, chair of the National Christian Foundation*
and chair of the Halftime Institute

Bigger Than Me is a wonderful reflection on faith and its power to transform lives. I came to know both Ward and his wife, Kris, as they faced large medical adversities. This inspiring treatise on the virtues of faith, hope, and charity (love) is a joy to read.

—*Greg Vercellotti, MD, professor of medicine at the University*
of Minnesota (and Ward's hematologist)

If you hang out with Ward Brehm long enough, you know you are with a genuine, fun-loving knucklehead who loves Jesus. And if he was a jerk in his youth (his description), you know for sure he is certainly a redeemed one who loves God, his family, friends, and most certainly the poor. *Bigger Than Me* is an honest story of one person's journey in discovering Jesus in a relevant way. I am inspired by Ward's story but even more inspired by the man.

—*Ralph Veerman, president of Veerman & Associates*

With humility, humor, and a sense of service to others, Ward Brehm tells his story, which ranges from Minnesota and business success to walking among tribesmen in rural Africa and entering the deepest halls of power in Washington, DC. Along the way, he found his purpose and now delivers his message. Take the ride.

—*Donovan Webster, explorer, freelance journalist, and author of* The Burma Road

Ward's book *Bigger Than Me* strongly exhorts us to lead with love and to earn the right to be heard. Ward has led a life of love, and he has certainly earned the right to be heard. So dive in to *Bigger Than Me*. You'll not only enjoy it but also be challenged by it.

—*Daniel Wordsworth, president and CEO of the American Refugee Committee*

Bigger Than Me is a great read! Deep in content and compulsively readable. All the elements of a life lived in full are here, including being a self-described jerk, an authentic journey of faith to Jesus, deeply revealing self-reflection, great quotes that you'll want to remember, and the centrality of surrender in reference to faith. Ward has a deftness of touch that leads to a most satisfying reading experience and ends so appropriately with thoughts on gratitude. I highly recommend this book.

—*E. Peb Jackson, Jackson Consulting Group, Colorado Springs, Colorado*

I never knew the old Ward Brehm, but I love the new one—the one who writes as he lives. He's funny, compassionate, turbo-charged, self-giving, generous, and occasionally deep! I love his low tolerance for religion and facades but high tolerance for authentic wrestling with the big issues. This book is his written DNA, expressed winsomely and movingly through the various crazy encounters that came about as he ditched religion and started following Jesus—the One who promised life to the full.

—*Simon Guillebaud, founder of Great Lakes Outreach, Burundi*

Ward Brehm has transformed my thinking and work at Opportunity International by allowing me to share his journey to a more vibrant and meaningful life filled with purpose, adventure, and contentment. *Bigger Than Me* explains the message of stewardship and intentional living and is the guidebook for creating a richer, fuller life focused on things that *really* matter.

—*Mark Thompson, chairman of Global Board of Directors, Opportunity International, and principal of Riverbridge Partners*

Bigger Than Me is a transparent self-assessment of a man who is making a big difference in Africa. This is a book that will provide spiritual and practical guidance for those looking for the something that is missing on what ought to be fulfilling lives.

—*Ambassador Linda Thomas Greenfield, former assistant secretary of state for Africa and ambassador to Liberia*

Ward weaves a compelling story about his transformational journey, and there are many important lessons to be learned here. His experiences and lessons learned have great relevance for anyone interested in leading a well examined life. I strongly recommend reading this book, *Bigger Than Me.*

—*Whitney MacMillan, chairman emeritus at Cargill*

Bigger Than Me demonstrates many ways each of us can be enlightened and self-explore with God being at life's center.

—*US Congressman Erik Paulsen*

My friend Ward Brehm took a long and circuitous route to find the position of "Jesus plus nothing." He has nearly arrived. I have read and heard literally hundreds of testimonials, but *Bigger Than Me* is the most Spirit-filled one I have read.

—*The Honorable Paul Magnuson, United States District Court judge*

Ward Brehm is an extraordinary individual who brings keen business acumen and a big heart to his work on behalf of the world's most vulnerable. *Bigger Than Me* is a must-read.

—*Raj Shah, president of the Rockefeller Foundation and former administrator of USAID*

Bigger Than Me

Ward Brehm

BroadStreet

PUBLISHING

BroadStreet Publishing® Group, LLC
Racine, Wisconsin, USA
BroadStreetPublishing.com

Bigger Than Me

Just when I thought I had all the answers,
God changed the questions

ISBN-13: 978-1-4245-5500-0 (hardcover)
ISBN-13: 978-1-4245-5501-7 (e-book)

Stock or custom editions of BroadStreet Publishing titles may be purchased in bulk for educational, business, ministry, fundraising, or sales promotional use. For information, please e-mail info@broadstreetpublishing.com.

Cover design by Chris Garborg | garborgdesign.com.
Interior design and typeset by Katherine Lloyd | theDESKonline.com.

Printed in China

17 18 19 20 21 5 4 3 2 1

This book is dedicated to:

Kris, my wife and the love of my life;
Andy, Mike, and Sarah Brehm,
their children to come ... and theirs;

My mom, Myke Brehm;

My mentors:
Doug Coe (1929–2017)
Arthur Rouner (1929–)
Monty Sholund (1920–2007)
Wheelock Whitney (1926–2016);

And to those among the poor in Africa,
who taught me how to really live.

Other Books by Ward Brehm

✦✦✦

Life Through a Different Lens

White Man Walking

(All author profits from Ward's books are given to help the poor in Africa.)

Contents

Foreword

I first met Ward Brehm in 2007, around a shared passion for helping the poor in Africa, and we instantly became friends.

In a world where more and more of what we do is based upon the urgent, Ward addresses the important. In *Bigger Than Me*, he tackles, with courage and unusual transparency, the significant topics of faith, money, aging, ego, mortality, success, and thankfulness.

Through highly personal and compelling stories, Ward relates how, at forty years of age, he realized that the American dream wasn't all it was cracked up to be. Having achieved career and material success, he found himself asking the age-old question, "Is this all there is?" His father's untimely death raised even more questions and prompted him to begin searching for more meaning in life.

In *The Purpose Driven Life*, I laid out a path for people to find their own unique purpose. At middle age, Ward was fortunate enough to travel to Africa where God allowed him to discover the purpose for his life. Rather than dull images of slideshow missionary trips, Jesus opened up an exciting new world of huge challenges and deep meaning. Ward got involved in things far bigger than himself.

Ever since, he has worked tirelessly as an advocate for the poor. Along the way, he has met with countless diplomats and African heads of state. And, in addition to being appointed by both Presidents G. W. Bush and Barack Obama to the United States African Development Foundation, Ward has acted as an unofficial ambassador of Jesus in Africa, the halls of Congress, and all across this country.

At the National Prayer Breakfast in 2008, I heard Ward present the keynote address. His authenticity, unique humor, and sincere faith made a significant impact on me and the thousands who heard him speak that morning. Later that year, President George W. Bush awarded Ward the Presidential Citizens Medal in the Oval Office.

In *Bigger Than Me,* Ward is refreshingly candid in detailing the way he has struggled with the important things in life, sharing experiences and lessons relevant to all generations.

From a businessman's perspective, Ward has a unique and often humorous take on the vast difference between the doctrine and dogma of religion and the freedom and adventure that comes when simply following Jesus. His thoughts on hypocrisy, prayer, the church, and why good things happen to bad people offer some compelling apologetic arguments to cynics, skeptics, and those at every level in their faith.

In today's world of instant everything, Ward allows readers to hit the pause button and reflect (a lost art) on things of greater significance. With a focus on faith, this book provides a first-person perspective and non-judgmental take on serious issues that most people agree are important but seldom have the time or space upon which to ruminate.

Bigger Than Me is for men and women who have experienced success and achieved many of their goals and who are now asking deep inside, *Is this all there is?* But it is also a book for all readers— young and old—who really aren't sure what true success looks like. This book will change your life if you pause long enough to contemplate its lessons.

Let it be so.

Rick Warren
May 2017

Introduction

We shall not cease from exploration
And the end of all our exploring
Will be to arrive where we started
And know the place for the first time.
—T. S. ELIOT

I've often said that if you want to hear God laugh out loud, all you need to do is tell Him your plans. I can say on pretty good authority I've provided Him some entertainment with mine.

God then needs to get your attention. In my experience, He'll begin by tossing a pebble into your life. If that doesn't work, He'll throw a rock. If you still haven't looked up, He'll heave a brick!

Africa was my brick.

In 1993, I wasn't looking up much—I was too busy living the dream. I was forty-two, had hit my version of the jackpot financially, and surpassed every personal goal I'd set for myself, and my life was a nice round of pats on the back, which translated to power and influence. What was there not to like?

I was doing fine. Yet why wasn't I happy beyond imagination? Why did I have this ominous sense that something big was missing? Could it be true that, like Stephen Covey's word picture, I had climbed the ladder of success only to find it leaning against the wrong wall?

During this time of my life, I lost my father. Reeling from the blow, I climbed on a plane and traveled to Africa. Something my pastor had asked me to do.

It was an odd request, at best; Sub-Saharan Africa was the last place guys like me tended to go unless it was on a five-star safari, and it wasn't something I was particularly eager to do. I never saw it coming: in the least likely place, I was destined to stumble on answers I couldn't have attained any other way.

In Africa, I encountered the poorest of the poor. People so poor that they couldn't pull themselves up by their bootstraps (because they didn't know what a bootstrap was, let alone have access to any). They simply had the imperative of living to see another day, another week, another bout with disease or hunger. Something in my heart gave way. Something in my soul came to life, and a new journey began.

This book characterizes the wisdom I've gained as I've entered the second half of my life. I've discovered there are others like me—men and women who have realized there should be something more to the picture and who have questioned the long-held assumptions on which they've built their lives.

I don't think that, with a single swipe of the hand, I should push aside everything I've ever built or accomplished. But I'm thrilled and encouraged to say that the second half of life has offered so much more than I'd been told. I've found that there are deeper, far more satisfying goals in life than those with which our culture entices us, and there were ways for me to make a course correction that didn't involve sweeping the past aside. I've been able to use all the lessons I've learned to build something new and far more meaningful than I ever imagined.

I'm not one to rebrand myself. When I returned from my eye-opening trip to Africa, I continued my stumbling and my occasional wrong turns, just like always and just like everybody. But I knew I was after something new, and that changed my reactions to life. When I did something that clashed with my new perceptions of life—or when I *failed* to do something—I found myself thinking, *This won't do; it's counterproductive to becoming the person I want to be. Here's another corner of me that needs renovation.* I now suspect that will always be the case.

I had no idea where my new journey would carry me. I only knew that it was a grand new adventure, and that God would be at the very center of it. I was going to have to learn how to be this different person, because it had taken me quite a while to become the old one. But I was resolute. I was determined to reset my default to dependence and to relate to God each day in a brand-new way. I wanted my life to be about things that were significant and lasting. I wanted to find my way out of the rat race and be more meaningful to the human race.

Back in 1994, I told this story in *Life through a Different Lens*. As I reread that book, the words still strike me as true. But I've traveled many a mile since then, metaphorically and literally. I've continued my trips to Africa on a regular basis—fifty-six visits and counting. I've continued my life back home with a renewed purpose. On both fields, I find that I've fallen short of the mark I'd like to leave as I edge closer to the finish line.

So, I have a few stories to tell. I'm not high on pontificating and telling other people how to live their lives. But I'm the world's foremost authority on me and the things that have worked or failed in my own life. So, in a spirit of humility—not of pushiness or self-righteousness—I hope to offer these observations of what has happened to me in the pursuit of a more significant second act.

Somewhere in the back of my mind, I always thought I would want to "give back" to society, to do some good. But I always thought it would be boring, like potluck casseroles in church basements followed by missionaries presenting slide shows of faraway places. I would never have predicted the exhilarating twists and turns my life would take when I was given a new path—a calling to something much bigger than I. I couldn't think of anything dull or ordinary when my heart was breaking: My mind wasn't on the ordinary during my visit to Masaka, Uganda, where I held the hands of a twenty-year-old mother of four, a victim of AIDS, as she sighed her final breath. I wasn't bored as two presidents, Bush and Obama, appointed me to the board of directors of United States African Development Foundation (USADF), whose goal is to deliver the poor from poverty through job creation. That's a vision that would energize any man or woman with a pulse. It's added life to my years, and—I would venture—years to my life.

My new path didn't end there. I've flown from Andrews Air Force Base three times as part of presidential delegations to my beloved continent. I've spoken at White House faith-based initiative conferences. I've become good friends with congressional leaders on both sides of the aisle. And I was asked to be the keynote speaker at the 2008 National Prayer Breakfast. Later that year, President Bush awarded me the Presidential Citizens Medal in the Oval Office.

I won't be disingenuous enough to suggest I don't feel a sense of pride in the experiences I've enjoyed these last few years. But I'm also being quite honest when I tell you that I've been deeply humbled rather than puffed up. I've been acutely aware that God orchestrated every circumstance, because there is simply no way I could have. I found that when I finally became involved with things far greater than my own self-interest, life became meaningful beyond anything I could have even imagined on my own.

I have another (hopefully) modest reason for sharing these experiences. I believe doing good things has gotten a bad rap. Somehow, we've bought into the lie that the good life is showy and dramatic and surrounded by the flashing bulbs of the paparazzi. What I've found is that the greatest adventure comes when we stop living for self, stop piling up personal achievements, and begin living for things that really matter. Nothing is actually duller, in the long run, than one more bag of money, one more business conquest, or one more round of pleasure with diminishing returns of satisfaction.

When I do good things—*any* good thing—I'm doing God's things. When I started living by that philosophy, that's when my life became truly compelling and wildly unpredictable. While I don't want to be overly dramatic, I'm not afraid to say that I was finally aligned with the purpose for which I am here.

I realize that, for some people, putting aside the pursuit of money, status, and joyless excitement might seem like too big a sacrifice. Our culture has taught us to view the word *sacrifice* in a negative way. We picture someone being thrown into a volcano, or we think that someone is trying to steal our money or time. But what I have discovered is that any true sacrifice I make, when done for the right purpose, is overwhelmed by what comes back my way: relationships, adventure, wisdom, a powerful sense of purpose and contentment, and on the list goes.

Finally, this book is an exercise in self-exploration. Enlightenment has been defined as knowing who you are and being able to tell the truth about it. This is my attempt to do just that. And for whom am I writing? I'm writing for anyone who wonders what life's road may hold when they seek God or God finds them. This includes those for whom religion is primarily cultural, those who have lost or abandoned their faith, or those who consider themselves skeptics and atheists—people who really aren't sure at all about this "God talk." Believe me, I understand your hesitation and promise that you won't be preached to, argued with, or manipulated emotionally. This is just my story, and I'm sticking to it.

Ward Brehm
January 2017

1

My Father's Gift

The Legacy of My Dad

❖

Whoever does not have a good father
should procure one.

—FRIEDRICH NIETZSCHE

One night a father overheard his son pray,
"Dear God, make me the kind of man my daddy is."
Later that night, the father prayed, "Dear God, make me
the kind of man my son wants me to be."

—ANONYMOUS

My dad was any number of things, depending on how you knew him. For me, he was a wonderful father, a wise and insightful mentor for a young guy like me who was trying to figure out the world.

My father was one of those people who, whenever his name came up, evoked the same two words every time: *great guy*.

Growing up, I showed no signs of being a "great guy" in the making. For me, the word was *troublemaker*. Neither of my parents said it, of course. Their point of view was, "Why is this good boy doing such naughty things?" Then they would apply the consequences of my actions. Neither of my parents were lenient. If I did the crime, I did the time. But once my "sentence" was over, it was over. Through whatever discipline came, I felt their affection for me. Two more words would eventually enter my vocabulary, though I didn't know them yet: *unconditional love.*

We use that phrase quite often these days. (If only we used the actual concept as freely.) I've become aware through talking to many people just how rare and wonderful it is to know one is loved without reservation, without conditions or clauses or limits. I know people who labored long and hard to earn the love of a parent, because they didn't receive it otherwise. But growing up in my home, it was as solid as the concrete beneath our floor. I never realized how rare and precious that upbringing was—my childhood world was the kind of world depicted in an episode of *The Adventures of Ozzie and Harriet.* Mom and Dad were a team and among the greatest blessings of my life.

Dad expressed his love in the form of unswerving belief, played out in constant encouragement. If his children were a stock, he would have invested all he had. And when I felt low and like a failure, he wouldn't let my emotions stay there. He may not have agreed with all that I did and all that I thought, and he'd tell me so. What wasn't in dispute was his all-out support. What I felt from him was that ancient, intangible thing expressed in certain Old Testament stories, that thing every child had a deep need to feel. I had his *blessing.*

As for his own life, I've already told you: great guy. He lived large, smiled his way through the world, avoided moodiness and dampened spirits. When life dealt him the proverbial poor hand, he handled it with charm, grace, and plenty of humor. Never resentment, never bitterness, never demands upon life or God or anyone else. As he saw it, there was a family to care for, and he had no time for self-absorbed tantrums.

He put us first and showed it by his presence. As a successful businessman, he was able to choose his own hours and be available to us. This meant more fun, more attention, more family adventures. And you might ask, "Well, if all this is true, why did he have two sons who were constantly getting into trouble?" I can only tell you we weren't acting out from any lack of parental attention. Sometimes boys will be boys, and if all goes well, they tire of their own comedy and find the right path.

My brother Steve and I tested the boundaries, but we knew we aspired toward our father's image. He set the tone for us, for example, in how to approach faith—quietly and loyally, to be worn in the heart and not on the sleeve, in the manner of the generation from which he sprung. He was a church man and a deacon, but he was never showy about it.

I knew I wanted to be big and strong like my dad when I grew up. I wanted his looks, his charisma, his way of commanding a room. He loved a good Manhattan or a single malt Scotch. He snuck a cigarette from time to time, though he thought it a secret. He loved the outdoors, being truly at home in the woods or at the lake, but he could fill an Oxford suit and English leather shoes like nobody's business. He was, anyone would agree, a man for all seasons.

Maybe I'm a little biased—I had only the one dad, after all. Maybe my memory has airbrushed the past and made it artificially rosy. Except that my impressions were confirmed, over and over, by men and women who came to me and said, "Your father was something special." There was Rick, the garage attendant at my office parking garage, who stopped me after a visit from Dad and said, "Do you realize how lucky you are to have such a wonderful dad?" I smiled and agreed but wanted to know what provoked his comment. My dad had been leaving and gotten into a conversation with him. Dad parked his car, sat down, and spent time with this man. "I know he must be an important man—I can tell that—but he made time for a guy like me."

There were lots of incidents like that. Dad seemed to accomplish plenty without ever hurrying. He had time for anyone who needed a bit of it. If it were possible to be the mayor of one's set of acquaintances, he would have won in a landslide every time.

One of the greatest lessons he taught me was personal responsibility. One sunny summer evening, just before I took off for college, I was at home alone with Dad. He asked me if I wanted to have a drink with him. Though I was entering manhood, this was a surprise—we both knew how much trouble I'd brought on myself in high school from sneaking alcohol. I told Dad yes but I was thinking, *Is this a trick question?*

Dad mixed a tall Scotch and soda for each of us, and we took our drinks out to the porch. He wanted to tell me how pleased and proud he was about my new place in life as a university student. He wanted me to have good grades, but he also wanted to recommend that I have my share of fun. *Okay,* I thought. *Now this is getting really strange.*

"These are going to be the best four years of your life," he said with a smile. "And they won't come back around." He touched on the fact that in a unique time like this, I'd have lots of freedom but relatively few responsibilities; a chance to give life a test-drive without the pressing burdens of career and family. I continued to sip my drink and wonder where we were going with all this. There had to be a catch.

Sure enough, his voice found a tone slightly more solemn, and he said, "Four special years. *Four.* Not five. Not six."

So, that was it. He was wanting me to know that four special years of college life were on him. He would write the checks, I would have the fun and the learning opportunities. After that, I was on my own 100 percent.

This was an example of his formula of love plus boundaries. I had his full support, but I also knew what was expected of me. The clarity of that served me well, as I had the time of my life in college, while also preparing myself for a future that would arrive right on time, like a European train. It wasn't too shocking to anybody that I chose the same career as my dad. I wanted the flexibility, the family time, and the opportunity to relate to people the way he did.

The few years we spent in the same office were special. We didn't actually do any business together, but the proximity was something I treasured and that I knew I wouldn't have forever. I'm grateful I could see this, so we could enjoy making a few memories together while we were both adults.

One of these had us cutting and splitting firewood with my brother Steve. I was in the midst of building a home out in the woods, and family was a great place to find cheap labor. One day, as we worked, I realized that my father was slowing down a bit. As we took a break, sitting together on stumps, I looked at him and thought, *My dad is sixty-six. He's not going to be doing this kind of thing forever.* It was a hard truth I needed to confront.

It was only a few days later that he reported a bit of pain in his ribcage. X-rays revealed a broken rib. Dad, anything but a hypochondriac, had no clue when or how he had done such a thing.

There was a new series of tests, and the results weren't pleasing. He hadn't done anything to break the rib. He had a rare and deadly disease: multiple myeloma, also known as bone cancer. As a stage-one patient, he had perhaps five years to live.

We were all devastated. How could it be? The problem with men like Dad is that they create an illusion of invulnerability. They seem bigger than life, capable of knocking down any obstacle. But indeed, it's an illusion.

Characteristically, nothing about Dad's demeanor changed. He laughed, told jokes, and focused on others. The doctors, of course, were simply new additions to his vast menagerie of friends. And he simply kept on keeping on, even as the descent grew steeper and did so more quickly than anyone anticipated.

Chemo wasn't doing much. There was an experimental trial with interferons at the Mayo Clinic, a last resort. But it, too, accomplished nothing. I vented, "We were told five years! That's hard enough, but why aren't we even getting that?"

To make the situation even more bitter, both my parents had

gone annually to a cancer detection clinic at the University of Minnesota. My father's condition had shown up four years earlier on a report, and an internist had missed it. When Dad's oncologist shared this miserable account with me, I was furious. I would get lawyers. I would make these people pay for the devastation to my family.

Meanwhile, my dad continued to slip away.

And then I realized something shocking: we'd been given a gift.

If we'd known four years earlier about the cancer, it would have changed everything about the way we all lived, particularly my parents. They'd been renting places in Florida for a number of years and enjoyed some of the best years of their marriage there. They finally bought their place in the sun in Vero Beach, Florida. If they'd known earlier about Dad's sickness, they wouldn't have had those carefree years. I'm not a fan of medical incompetence, but I have to admit that sometimes there's grace in not knowing.

Dad fought his way toward the final rounds of the battle. He didn't give up. The doctors made it clear that they'd stopped all treatment—the outcome was assured—but my father never let that sink in. He talked about my future plans and included himself. He seemed to enjoy his days the same as if they were unnumbered. My mom was nothing short of heroic. From the onset she was determined to be Dad's primary caretaker. Despite the shock and heartbreak, she always kept up a positive front and kept her anguish, frustration, and despair from the family. She handled this disaster with patience, courage, and enormous grace. A huge gift to our family.

Then one day Dad developed pneumonia. They actually call it the cancer patient's best friend, with its grim mercy. Of course, his immune system was basically nonfunctioning by this time, and he had to be hospitalized. We gathered outside his room, where a doctor quietly explained that Dad would probably leave us sometime during the night. He simply didn't know Dad, who woke up the next day feeling great, with no signs of infection. The staff were dumbfounded. "Your dad is a great guy," one of them told me.

The new prediction was that he actually had a few months to live. When we gathered around his bed, you wouldn't have thought anyone was particularly sick. We were laughing and telling stories, and he was at his best. The door opened, and the primary physician stood before us.

"Hey, Doc," my dad said. "I'm tired of this bed. Could you give me some kind of a schedule on when I'm going to get better and can get back to normal?" We all looked at our feet a little awkwardly, because we knew there were limits to everything—even my father's buoyant confidence.

The doctor, who of course was a great friend of a great guy by now, said, "Ed, you're not going to get any better. This cancer is going to kill you, and it won't be too long until that happens."

The room was silent. We looked at Dad, who said, "Well, that's a bummer!"

It was the moment when reality truly set in—for all of us. Love and many other emotions were heavy in the atmosphere, and we all began to speak without euphemisms and evasions. "It's been a great ride," Dad said. "I've been blessed with a family that kept me happy, and I've had way more than my share of wonderful experiences. They had to end sometime."

His acceptance seemed to punctuate the whole experience, and he departed that very evening. There was no particular medical explanation. I think he calmly and gracefully let go. I also think that he did so out of love and concern for his family. He didn't want them halting their lives to care for or grieve over him. He needed to be out of their way, the sooner to move through the mourning process and resume what really matters in life.

As I said my goodbyes, feeling profoundly deprived of his presence, I grew up. I'd always known that dads aren't forever. I was thirty-eight, and he was sixty-seven. There was a quarter-century between us. Even so, I hadn't known how much it would hurt. I hadn't considered what it would mean to wake up each morning and realize he wasn't there for me anymore. I'd never realized it was possible to hurt so deeply. I hadn't ever faced anything remotely close to such a loss. Still relatively young, I'd fashioned myself—in his manner—as the captain of my own fate, the master of all I surveyed. And here was something I couldn't master.

What I've come to realize was that the depth of my loss was a gift. In leaving me, Dad bequeathed me one final and priceless treasure. I had to come to the end of myself; I had to realize there were things in life I couldn't handle with nonchalance. I was a jerk—a nice guy kind of jerk perhaps, but even so, a guy severely in need of humbling.

The gift of my father was ultimately a gift from another Father, and it must be so because of the timing of these events. Only a few years later, I was climbing on a plane to Africa. The loss of Dad, coupled with the aftershock of Africa, provided a one-two punch that remade me from the inside out. Only God can coordinate the schedules by which these things come together in our lives. Dad's death forced me to confront mortality; Africa forced me to confront meaning.

Now, as the years have passed, I don't really recall the physical devastation of my father's final months. What I remember is the booming laugh, just as if I'd heard it yesterday. I recall the presence, the encouragement, and the love, and I realize that even as a relatively immature forty-two-year-old, I was learning something that truly mattered in life. He taught me how to be a father, husband, friend, and member of the human race. And while I miss being able to reach out and touch his shoulder or get a bear hug, I still feel him among us. I feel his pride over his children and grandchildren. And I know that he's no further away than the eternity we will share.

2

Metamorphosis

Can God Change a Jerk?

Maybe as we move towards spiritual maturity,
we come to the same conclusion as Job that it's less
about possessions, order and success, and more about
an ability to live with uncertainty, loss and mess?
—SIMON GUILLEBAUD

When I was forty, life had left me dizzy. Nothing had prepared me for living at a faster and faster pace until I seemed to have very little control over my own life. I was doing well financially, and I had made the climb of success. But I found myself in a roller coaster compartment with no steering wheel and no brake—only the instinct to hang on tight.

Like others, I looked to technology—all these new advances and breakthroughs—to help me get better control of things. I bought the most expensive smartphone I could find and downloaded every scheduling, organizational, and financial app there was in the hopes that these things would keep me calm as well as connected. Yet each one only created more urgency and obligations and drained me more.

My to-do list was growing longer and my time was growing shorter. I had a general, ongoing impression of sensory overload. I'm the kind of Type A personality who likes to attend to the details in his life in a thoughtful and orderly way. I couldn't do that with life throwing those details at me faster and harder. It was like standing in a batting cage with more and more pitching machines pointed at me.

Still, I could get things done. What bothered me, down deep, was the nagging feeling of what was slipping under the radar. There wasn't a stray moment left in my day for general reflection, much less thinking about God or the spiritual dimension of things. By any normal standard, I was "successful"—very much so. The world of business hadn't been a particularly hard nut for me to crack. I'd always figured I could get to the top. What I hadn't predicted was how the top would get to *me*. The great irony of the American ideal is that it would have us believe that success makes us captains of our own fate. In fact, it does no such thing; the captain simply has a greater, more complex, and more clamorous ship to guide.

Today, they call such things "first world problems." As in, "Yeah, right—you have three square meals a day, fresh water, and a roof, so you have to *find* something to worry about." I get that. Still, the fact remained that I was exhausted and spiritually empty. The P word—*purpose*—was coming up more and more. I was trading a vast portion of my time on earth for this list of business accomplishments. Was it a good trade?

In addition to questioning my life's purpose, I had just suffered one of the most profound losses of my life. My father had passed away, and I was unprepared in every way for the grief I felt. It didn't seem like such a bad idea to escape the places and faces of my world for a brief time. Stepping out of the first world into a totally different environment might be a way to absorb the shock.

And that's how Africa came into my world and changed me forever. In my home of Minneapolis, a group of churches, including mine, was beginning a mission to parts of Africa that were in crisis. I knew there was hunger, warfare, disease, and despair in that distant place, and something in my spirit said, *You need to be on that plane. You need to experience that world, that alternate reality, for yourself.*

People had told me that Africa changes you deep down. They were right, but there was no way I could anticipate *how* right. In the same way, when you're about to become a parent for the first time, people say, "This is going to change your life." You nod and you know they're right, but *still* you're blindsided, no matter how many Lamaze classes you take and books you read.

By the usual standards of success, my cup was overflowing at the time I went to Africa. All I can tell you is that Africa knocked my cup over. And it's not just me. Over the years, I've had the privilege of seeing other business and political leaders go to the so-called dark continent, only to have the light come on in their lives.

Whenever I relate my story verbally, it's at this point people ask me, "Why Africa? Why not across the railroad tracks, on the other side of town? Why not over the river into the worst places in Mexico?" There are some tragic sights to be seen in those places, no question. But with Africa, I believe it has something to do with *capacity*. I would explain it this way: Go to rural Africa—you choose the region—and you'll find a society of human beings living lives of deep difficulty on so many fronts. The more you talk to them, the greater and more heartrending the challenges you find. These individuals have no social station, no status, no titles, no possessions, and no real hope of anything ever being different.

I saw a world of people like that, and seemingly every one of them—hungry, poor, and often sick—possessed a rich, calm spirituality and peace of mind that I, with all my temporal blessings, was craving. You can fill in your pet truisms about wealth versus the simple life here. I've heard them and so have you. But seeing people living in extreme poverty yet leading joyous lives is a paradigm blaster. Here were "the least of these," as Jesus called them in Matthew, and from the bottom of the world's social ladder they could teach me—a few thousand rungs upward—about *contentment*. And they could teach it without saying a word.

The woman carrying the water jar three miles from the river.

The man with the joyous laugh who also had open sores with flies buzzing around them.

The children, owning no toys and having fun anyway.

I could hear the voice of Jesus saying, "This is how I've told you to come to me—like one of these children. Without finding what these little ones have, you cannot enter the kingdom of heaven."

I saw before me joyous children—but I also saw a childlike capacity in adults. It only followed to think about what I saw in the mirror. Did I possess that simplicity of essence, that natural honesty? Actually, honesty now suggested this word to me: *jerk*.

I came here as a jerk, I told myself. The stillness of the souls before me were a reflecting glass allowing me to see deep into myself. It was an ugly picture I couldn't tolerate, and it was going to change. Whatever the price, I would pay it. I couldn't live with the legacy of receiving countless blessings only to become a dime-a-dozen American jerk.

I believe I did change, beginning then and there, though I'm sure there are some who know me and would offer alternative viewpoints. The better statement would be that God changed me, because I know it's impossible to re-create my basic nature. The renowned expert on me—my wife, Kris—concurs, adding the corollary that I'm "often wrong but seldom in doubt." Over these two decades, she's commented on seeing a different me: a bit less self-absorbed, materialistic, and arrogant.

While the change process began in me when I realized I came to Africa as a jerk, if I had to choose one transforming moment, I'd pick the moment when I met a little village girl in a remote part of north central Ethiopia called Antsokia Valley, which had been hard hit in the mid-1980s by a terrible famine. This little girl was six, the same age as my own Sarah. I looked at this little one and couldn't help but compare the two girls, separated by so much more than an ocean. She was a beautiful child, and something about her opened up my heart. There was nothing tangible that happened, nothing to make a great story. All I know is that something within me finally gave way. Later that evening, around a bonfire in those hills, I gave up all that I was and all I'd been clutching about my old way of life. I offered the balance of that trip to God—and, if He wanted it, the balance of my life. Immediately, as I made this transaction in my spirit, a powerful, all-embracing sense of peace flooded across me. One little girl, in the hands of God, had opened the dam.

I was experiencing that moment of discovery when one finds that the world does not revolve around himself, that what I perceived as needs were merely wants, and that my life goals were superficial and material. I wanted money, but I also wanted admiration, fame, power, and, if at all possible, to be the king of my own private universe, god of my own cosmos. I knew there was one true God, but He would have to fit into *my* plan accordingly. This was the moment when one grasps the power of the first sentence in Rick Warren's book, *The Purpose Driven Life*: "It's not about you."

To have ever thought it was about me, to have ever had those goals, to have ever been so arrogant—the only word that fit was *jerk*.

To announce full-scale change is to encounter skepticism, even cynicism, from those around us, including people who love us. I don't know why this is. Perhaps some have given up on such change in their own lives, and someone else's hope shines too brightly in the dim rooms they've accepted for themselves. Perhaps they've heard it all before, only to see a failure to launch. There are no statues erected to honor naysayers and critics. But you hear from them. In my case, many of my peers asked, "Why would you want to change? There's nothing wrong with you."

I replied that, in fact, I didn't want to change. While I knew something was missing, I was happy enough with my life on an everyday basis. I was surrounded by good things to enjoy: family, a satisfying career, friends, and fun. While my life felt full, I didn't. That sense of "missing-ness" was small but persistent. The voice calling me to change didn't seem to come from the place where all my blessings were stored; it seemed to come from somewhere else. My soul was like a fine old house with a hidden room behind the bookcase, and there was a voice in that room trying to communicate some message to me. Late at night, lying in bed and reflecting on the day, I would begin to hear that voice again.

My own experience of being a jerk has led me to what I call my "jerk theory": when someone lives their life without some deeply humbling experience—something that drives them to their knees, whether it's the loss of a beloved person, a divorce, a great failure, or a deep illness—they become a jerk. The more someone achieves without humility and the older they grow without their arrogance being checked, the bigger a jerk they become.

Africa was my humbling experience. It brought me to my knees. Africa showed me that everything I thought I knew was wrong. Just when I thought I had all the answers, Africa changed the questions. In Africa, the hard-and-fast rules are soft and slow. The things of epic importance, weighing down your heart, suddenly don't register. The crazy pace at which you've been living suddenly looks not like a status symbol but a Saturday morning cartoon that's a bit embarrassing. And the world's greatest secret—the search for the meaning of life—seems to be written on the face of everyone you meet.

There's a line in the film *I Am Legend*, a movie about the near end of the world when only a few people are still alive. A woman says that the world had formerly been a loud and busy place, and the more it became those things, the less God's voice could be heard. "The world is quieter now," she says. "You just have to listen and you can hear God's plan." That's what I believe people experience in Africa. It's something like the end of the world. Away from all my mess, all the noise and rush, I was able to hear what God had been trying to say all along. He had never stopped speaking; I simply let His voice be drowned out.

But not these people. These Africans were hearing God all the time: there was a sense that He embraced their singing and their prayers, which are so genuine and simple and honest. His presence could be felt powerfully when they gathered to lift up His name. And His reality could be perceived when they're doing almost anything else. These people came to God as little children, not as philosophers or theologians or connoisseurs of church life. They merely basked in His joy. I came to Africa with plenty of worldly treasures, but I knew I'd found my pearl of great price.

It wasn't an easy experience for me, confronting the face of selfishness in my life. A face, of course, can be altered with cosmetics or surgery. I know I often continue to put myself first. But the real issue for me was that that face reflected the emptiness inside me. Admitting there's a void within was a hard thing. But I believe God loved that void. It's the place where He announced Himself then, once welcomed, was able to make a home.

When I returned from Africa, my focus had shifted. I worked on being less Ward centered and more God centered. I tried setting my heart on eternal things rather than material things. And I began to see how I could find more capacity for my life, more margin to devote to things that mattered, and more selfless presence in the moment.

Besides my first journey to Africa, only one other event in my life humbled me so drastically: the death of my father shortly before this trip. Now, I was coming home as a forty-two-year-old who, before leaving, had thought he had all the answers—but upon my return home, I was one who had all the questions. One thing I knew, however: I would go back to Africa. I had bonded with its needs. These people had done so much for me without even knowing it; I would do my best to return the favor. Turning away toward the new me and forgetting this continent would only be self-absorption in another insidious form. I needed this place, and I felt it needed me too—along with anyone I could take with me. I wanted to see its effect on others, to see their faith challenged and their capacities for reflection transformed in the way mine had been.

There are so many reasons Africa has this power to initiate change in people. During my experience, I knew it was a place where I had no power. I could bring my sense of order and need for control, but they wouldn't help me. There were few places in America I could go where I wouldn't be, in some way, in charge. But in the hills and plains so far away, none of my credentials meant a thing. I had no strings to pull. It was control-freak detox, and it was very disconcerting. I went where others decided rather than setting my agenda. I ate what was given to me rather than choosing from a menu. This in itself was a humbling experience.

Yet the lack of control became comfortable. It was nice not to be carrying such a burden every moment of my existence, to have a holiday from playing god of my own cosmos. My mind was freed up to observe, to reflect, to perform tasks that had been denied it for too long. My spirit was engaged rather than caged. It seemed to me that I was really living for a change and that I was "all there," devoted to the time and the moment. This was a me I didn't know very well, but I was pleased to make his acquaintance and wanted to know him much better. Of course, there was the matter of my faith during this experience. Was faith necessary to encourage me to change? Did this transformation have to be about God? Couldn't I just come back to the States as a better person, without giving all of myself to Him? I had grown up in and around church, but I had strong skepticism about organized religion. A mover and shaker like me couldn't find too much appeal in dependency upon anything, let alone faith. Jesus seemed to favor strugglers and stragglers, and that was fine. But I was making my own way. I also had my suspicions that religion was some kind of control mechanism, the "opiate for the masses," as Karl Marx called it.

Even so, I had sought God in my tentative way. I took the church's prescription for a faithful life, without much effect. It seemed to me that *trying* to attain faith just pushed me further away from it. It was like trying to have a crush on a girl I wasn't attracted to; all that happened was I was reminded of why I wasn't attracted. Faith can't be bought, earned, or gathered—when it's pursued in those ways, you just end up further away from it than when you started.

But somehow, in Africa, faith was in the air that I breathed. Something I once couldn't summon was now impossible to avoid. Because of Africa? No, because of Africa humbling me. Sometimes our reach exceeds our grasp until we try it from a low position. It wasn't that I now opened that door of faith—it swung open before me. I didn't find God, but He came and found me. And this humbled me all the more.

I'd always had questions about how all that worked—all those stories of people "finding Jesus" in prison or on the other end of some terrible crisis. Something about the jailhouse conversion seemed awfully convenient. People had their fun, then hid behind God when it came time for the consequences.

I'm less cynical about these things now. What I lacked was an understanding of what it means to be broken. When people have their world knocked out from under them, there is a prism of humility through which the spectrum of grace shines in a beautiful way. To put it more simply, you can't fill a cup that is already full. There are certain situations in life that are more capable of knocking over that cup, no matter how tight our grasp upon it may be. I was broken in more ways than one, having lost my father and then, through this experience in Africa, my bearings.

I look back at the old version of me without regrets. I was what I was, and the old me provided the ingredients for who I am now. My vision of life and faith now is all the brighter for the background from which it emerged. I feel I'm seeing life through a new and more deeply focused lens. But I wasn't eager to give up the old lens. I figured I'd live the good life, or what I thought that was, until I reached a ripe old age when I could embrace things like wisdom and faith and reflection.

But after that trip, my view of these things was turned topsy-turvy. Faith and reflection *were* the good life. The rest was no life at all. I saw Jesus followers around me in tighter definition through this new lens. They weren't the somber, pious types I had believed they would be—they had purpose, contentment, and a very nice measure of plain old fun.

The greatest consequence of that experience in Africa was that I redefined how I would spend the rest of my life. I would be devoted now to things other than building the walls of my personal kingdom. I wanted to find out what really mattered in life and pursue those things with the new capacity I perceived God had given me. One of those things, I knew, was Africa. This trip was not a one-time event; it was, as they say in the movies, the beginning of a beautiful friendship. I would think of and pray for Africa every day. I would invest my business and organizational skills toward finding positive solutions for the challenges there, and in my home country I would become an advocate for all kinds of ministry and service to that place.

There was so much more to pursue as well. What was my new life going to look like? What would family, career, church, and other things look like through this new lens? The questions kept coming, but I now knew they were part of a grand adventure.

3

Losing My Religion

And Finding a Person Named Jesus

> Jesus transcends religion because he is the incarnation
> of all that is true, good, loving, gentle, tender, thoughtful,
> caring, courteous, and selfless. Jesus does not want
> you to become a Christian. He wants you to become
> a new creation! There is a great difference between the two.
>
> —RICHARD HALVERSON, FORMER US SENATE CHAPLAIN

Some who are reading this may have a deep faith in Jesus. But I'm certain others have no particular connection to Jesus. They may see Him from the perspective of some other religion. Or they simply may be agnostic or atheistic.

Of course, your spiritual choices are completely up to you, and I personally resent the force-feeding of beliefs. I would like to share some perhaps "outside the box" thinking about the person of Jesus, and I only ask for an open mind and heart. What have you got to lose?

We'll probably agree that few people in Western culture begin with a blank slate when it comes to opinions about Jesus. Nearly everyone has a strong stance. Where can we find common ground?

One area of agreement is the question of Jesus' impact. Most people would agree with my statement that His life and teachings have been globally and historically influential. Jesus is universally acknowledged as the greatest leader in history. Certainly, He's been the subject of more books than any other person—even with only three years of ministry in His lifetime.

But Jesus had little access to the tools of influence. He never had a public relations director. He had no real possessions, and He never traveled outside of the obscure little region where He spent His three years of ministry. He wrote no manifestos, and He never held public office. He simply walked from town to town, spoke, and showed love for people. He did manage to upset the religious and legal leaders by turning conventional wisdom and belief on their heads.

Could it be that Jesus was just the right guy at the right time? That He supplied public demand? Not at all. His people were expecting a messiah, but one who was a fire-breathing, sword-wielding soldier who would lead an uprising against the Roman Empire and restore the nation of Israel to prominence. They wanted a king, not a rabbi full of puzzling sayings. They wanted someone from the upper crust, not someone who socialized with outcasts. And when they found out about His reluctance to fit that template, they turned on Him.

Strangest of all, Jesus died a humiliating and painful death befitting a criminal. The cross was the ultimate badge of shame, a ticket to history's refuse bin. By all rights, He should have been forgotten within a few weeks. Yet we recognize Him twenty centuries later as the most influential figure in world history.

When I ponder the greatest tribute any person could receive as a legacy, do I consider the Washington Monument? Michelangelo's *David*? The Lincoln Memorial? All of these commemorate great men. So where is the Jesus Memorial? It's rooted so deeply in our culture that we don't even think about it: the calendar.

Think about this. We halted time and started it over, based on the assumed year of Jesus' birth. I came eventually to a moment when that struck me as an astounding fact. And it didn't fit my rather ho-hum conception of Jesus. I realized my need to pause and think a little harder about this man who lived so long ago.

I began with this assumption: the way most of us view Jesus is based on where we were born and who raised us. We see Jesus just as we were taught to see Him. If you were born in the American South, you might be a Baptist. If you're from Minnesota, you might be a Lutheran. And if you're from California, you might be a hedonist (just kidding). If you were born in India, you'd likely live and worship as a Hindu. If you're from Israel, you'd probably be a Jew, and if you are from Saudi Arabia, you'd probably be a Muslim. All of these varied backgrounds result in Jesus meaning many different things to many different people.

Religious beliefs should be investigated with supreme care, chosen, and owned. But most frequently, they come to us through osmosis. We soak in the assumptions of the crowd.

It's no different with feelings about Jesus. You might identify with Him profoundly or feel nothing at all about Him, but your starting point is likely to be an inherited stance.

Notice I said *starting point*. If I've been describing you—if you're still in the general neighborhood of the beliefs you inherited, my request is for you to very briefly put them aside. You can always pick them up later and carry on. Just for the moment, why not consider a new way of thinking about Jesus?

My proposition is that people not only accept the group-sanctioned Jesus, but they also give Him a makeover to match their world view. In other words, people may like Jesus, but they like Him better when He can be customized to their preferences. He wants to transform them, but they're the ones who try and change him to fit into their specific paradigms.

So customizing Jesus becomes Jesus Plus. For example, there's Jesus Plus Political Conservatism or Jesus Plus Liberalism. There's Jesus the Baptist and Jesus the Presbyterian. Jesus can be reimagined in an infinite variety of flavors. But I need to remember that Jesus wasn't even an American! He wasn't a Republican. He wasn't a Democrat. He wasn't a Catholic or Protestant.

I'll take it a little farther. *Jesus wasn't a Christian.* He was, in fact, Jewish by faith and creed. Therefore, when I define Jesus according to my own cultural beliefs, I put Him in a box. I reduce who He is, so that Jesus Plus actually turns out to be Jesus Minus the individual limitations I put on him. When asked what people thought of the term *born-again Christian*, most nonreligious Americans respond with terms like *hypocritical, small-minded, mean-spirited, caustic,* and *angry ideologues*. To me, this is yet another shocking reality, because it shows there are vast throngs of people, all claiming to be followers of Jesus, who fail to live or speak in the way He asked them to live or speak.

How does that happen? I've been around long enough to notice that the followers of Jesus often are less like Him than like the hypocritical religious leaders who infuriated Him.

We can be so far removed from Jesus that, in addition to being toxic Christians, we often turn Jesus into a storybook character. Rodney Howard-Browne, in his book *Seeing Jesus as He Really Is*, makes this point well. Jesus wasn't the soft-voiced, fragile young man with the lamb under his arm and the preference for speaking Elizabethan English. If He were among us now, He'd still be clashing with the religious powers that be. And a great number of us wouldn't like Him at all, particularly those of us who claim to like Him the most right now. "Religious tradition tries to keep him on the cross or in the crib," Howard-Browne writes. "In the cross or in the crib, but not in the crowd—not out where he can change the way the world lives and loves."[1] Our current religious leaders might likely be at the head of the mob running Him out of town.

We handle Jesus by toning Him down, by making Him fit for polite company. But He was never mild or dull. He wasn't really "religious" at all, though we depict Him as the great voice of the status quo and the doctrines of the moment. But as British author Dorothy Sayers put it,

Those who crucified Jesus did not, to do them justice, do so because he was a bore. Quite the contrary, he was too dynamic to be safe. It has been left for later generations to muffle up that shattering personality and surround him with an atmosphere of tedium. We have effectively pared the claws of the lion of Judah, certified him 'meek and mild,' and made him a house cat for pale priests and pious old women.[2]

Religion that emphasizes doctrine and dogma can feel like a slow-drip feed of guilt and obligation. Where is the adrenaline of Jesus? Where is the heart-pounding adventure of following a revolutionary new way to live: eyes set on the goal; finishing the race; living life not for trophies, recognition, or self-fulfillment but for something much bigger than self? Why would we want to tone down the idea of living passionately in the manner of Eric Liddell, the Olympic athlete whose story is told in the film *Chariots of Fire*? When questioned on the purpose of running, he answered, "When I run, I feel God's pleasure."

In his biblical paraphrase, *The Message*, Eugene Peterson offers a short introduction to Luke's Gospel. He says that Jesus came to earth to show love for every single person, regardless of sect, religion, race, or ability. Thus, we find Jesus ministering both to the "respectable" people as well as the outcasts—the prostitutes, the criminals, the tax collectors, the lepers. In one of His provocative parables, Jesus cast a Samaritan, a member of a totally alienated sect, as the hero on the road to Jericho. Jesus saw a world in which no one should be an outcast; everyone could be a hero based on their heart rather than their social status. The only true villains were those within the religious community who refused to choose love over law.

I often hear people talk about the importance of making a decision for Christ. Jesus never told us to "decide" for Him. He told us to *follow* Him. I define that as obeying Him, and I believe it makes quite a difference. He isn't about a set decision but a course of action. He isn't a church-sanctioned "bowling trophy" that gathers dust on a shelf. He's the sounding trumpet of a new life that turns out to be God's aggressive, outrageous love taking form among us, cutting a swath through society and all its ingrained misconceptions.

Jesus often spoke about Himself as a shepherd, which makes the rest of us His sheep. He said, "I have other sheep that are not of this sheep pen. I must bring them also. They too will listen to my voice, and there shall be one flock and one shepherd" (John 10:16). For years, I read those words and assumed that Jesus was talking about other religions—the Hindu pen on this side, the Buddhist one on that side. Then I realized *I* was the sheep in the other pen. He meant me! I am the latest transformational work of Jesus. Yielding to Him means exchanging my poor, fading life for His vibrant, provocative one on a daily basis.

Jesus didn't compartmentalize the world the way we tend to do. He recognized no social boundaries. He invited Matthew (also known as Levi, the tax collector) into His inner circle, where he would be on public display with the rest of the disciples. Why would that matter? Because at that time, tax collectors were despised as turncoats—greedy opportunists who collaborated with the invading Romans by extorting a little extra money for themselves as they collected the taxes.

Tax collectors were hated—but Jesus befriended them and dined in their homes. Rather than being the meek and mild advocate of traditional values, He was seen as disrespectful of beloved customs and beliefs. He was a threat to the stability of both Jewish and Roman authority.

Jesus walked a perilously fine line perfectly, on the one hand obeying the wishes of God while on the other hand having overwhelming compassion for those who didn't obey those wishes. That's a highly attractive code of conduct in my eyes and reason enough for me to follow Him. He was having none of the religious leaders and their teachings as they turned God's ancient laws into a series of whips and yokes.

I can read the Old Testament and understand how God gave His laws out of love, but people used them oppressively as tools of power and subjugation. They promoted a society that turned a blind eye to poverty and hunger, to widows and the sick, to anyone disenfranchised—even to the Roman soldiers themselves. Jesus was the essence of a revolutionary, following God's laws and revealing the love behind them while condemning the abuses heaped upon them by the people claiming to safeguard them. Jesus was the essence of a revolutionary. How did we make Him so boring?

Author and speaker Nathan Foster has done some thinking about how he would have gone about Jesus' job if it had been left up to him. What if it was his mission to bring a message to change the world, establish a kingdom on earth, and launch the reign of God's love? Foster says he'd hit the street and get to work with a sense of urgency. He'd go after the power structure, establish a formal organization, raise money, build buildings and schools, and spread the message to the largest possible audiences. He would single out the thought leaders and difference-makers, and set up fund-raising dinners. He'd enmesh himself in the powers that be.

Yet Jesus took His time, doing nothing worth recording for His first thirty years, then wandering for three more years in a little cluster of nobodies. Who else would possibly have chosen that strategy? Yet the long-term results are staggering.

Attempts to hijack Jesus to conform to religious and cultural dogma and beliefs can fuel misunderstandings, wars, division, hatred—in a word, alienation, both from God and one another. To put it another way, we quickly learned how to take Jesus and use Him as the very kind of tool of oppression that He came to condemn. I can assure you that when alienation is precipitated, it doesn't trace back to Jesus. Something has been warped or distorted along the way.

As a result of this imbedded alienation, I have stopped referring to myself as a Christian. After all, the term *Christian* appears in Scripture just three times, and Jesus never asked anyone to become a Christian. What He did give us were the words: "Follow me" (Matthew 4:19; Mark 1:17; Luke 5:27; John 1:43; 21:19). So, I prefer to define my own spiritual journey that way and consider myself simply a follower of Jesus. In this season of life, as I think about what is really important to me, I need to lose my religion and learn what it truly means to follow Jesus. There's a simplicity to that, and I find it empowering. I don't have volumes of creeds and laws to learn. I just follow the leader. Jesus told His disciples to do neither more nor less than practicing what He taught. And in its essence, what He taught is really fairly simple.

Jesus never even said, "Worship me." The life of a sheep is to go where the shepherd guides. Trust the shepherd. Depend totally upon him. And in doing these things, the sheep is finding its true worship, a form that fits its life and capabilities perfectly.

I must also admit, however, that genuine trust and obedience are much more difficult than what passes for worship these days. I can "worship" without sincerity. I can leave the place of worship and change nothing about how I live.

Obedience to Jesus, however, leaves no opportunity for going through the motions. It places me in the way of messy tasks: caring for the supposedly unworthy, the sinners, the outsiders, the people whose paths I would least likely cross otherwise. Obedience humbles. It transforms. It's not a lifestyle that accumulates new friends.

Jesus once said that healthy people don't need doctors—sick people do. And He was calling on all of us to be doctors of caring. If that means losing my religion, I'm ready to do so. What a surprise when we go to church to see Jesus, and then He leads us right out of the building and into the places of highest need.

For the record, my pastor and close buddy, John Ross, gets that. In closing each Sunday worship service, he says, "Now that our worship together has come to an end, our *service* can begin."

Amen. (Which simply means, "I agree.")

4

Prove It

Some Thoughts for Skeptics

❖

An atheist is someone with no invisible means of support.

—Archbishop Fulton Sheen

Belief and confusion are not mutually exclusive. I believe that
belief gives you a direction in the confusion. But you don't
see the full picture. That's the point. That's what faith is—you
can't see it. It comes back to instinct. Faith is just up the street.
Faith and instinct, you just can't rely on them. You have to beat
them up. You have to pummel them to be sure that they can
withstand it, to make sure they can be trusted.

—Bono

Like any thinking adult, I had to come to grips with the "God
question." I was raised to believe in God; I believe most people
in my generation were. But there comes a time when we have to
call into question the ideas we've always assumed to be true—particularly the big ideas. And God certainly qualifies as a "big idea."

My atheist or agnostic friends tend to point to one great reason for not believing: lack of proof. Point taken. But for me, this is
the very reason we call this thing *faith*. Faith isn't necessary when
there's proof. But it seems to be necessary a great many other times.

I also have friends who point to objections far more personal—
they've had some negative experience with a church, a pastor, or a
religious hypocrite. They've seen people with, in Jonathan Swift's

words, "just enough religion to make them hate, but not enough to help them love one another."[1]

And these friends of mine have simply stopped investigating that greatest of all questions: What happens when we die?

I've seen stories of nonbelievers such as C. S. Lewis, who had no belief and no desire for any, reluctantly became a follower of Jesus because he couldn't deny that all things, once he honestly considered them, pointed to God. Frank Morison, a young lawyer, thought he would do the world a favor by disproving the resurrection; he succeeded only in demonstrating to himself that the resurrection is not mythology or legend but well-established history. He documented his findings in the book *Who Moved the Stone?*

If we can't prove there is a God, it's just as hard to disprove His existence.

Or maybe it depends on what we consider proof. I've seen the majesty of the dawn breaking over the San Juan Mountains and the sun fading over a Pacific horizon. At those moments, the reality of God seems more than certain to me. I can't behold the beauties of this world and ignore the evidence of grand and glorious design.

Everything in nature has its scientific basis and can be quantified by so many molecules in motion or principles of physics. But what about the emotional release I feel? What about our human impulse to cry out to God or to create works of art? Can science speak to those?

My journey of faith began with the idea that the life of Jesus, whose memorial is the calendar itself that divides history between "before Christ" and "in the year of our Lord," was a life worth looking into. His story, as told in the New Testament, led me to conclude that you can't make this stuff up. The narrative's peculiarities simply made it more compelling and gave it the ring of truth. No man would claim to be the Son of God unless he was a liar, insane, or indeed the Lord.

For people in my culture, the problem isn't that we don't know that story; it's that we're *too* familiar with it. It's the nativity scene of Christmas, the cross of Easter, and a few old paintings of a meek and mild Jesus. Familiar things become invisible to us—they become parts of life's passing scenery. History's central moment became a dull cultural backdrop.

But on a journey to Africa, I came to a village where the name of Jesus had never been heard. My companion, Reverend John Lodinyo, preached to the local tribe. As he began telling who Jesus was, the listeners turned their backs—in their culture, you don't speak of a son while his father yet lives. But their ears were still functioning, and the people became more interested. "This Jesus sounds like a good man," one said. "Bring Him here so that we may discuss."

Reverend Lodinyo smiled and said that Jesus had died. Again, the group turned away. They had thought this was about a hero—heroes don't die, particularly if his father is a god! Foolishness.

Lodinyo knew how to handle such a conversation. Patiently, affably, he explained the plan of the Father who sent His Son to die for *people*. A savior. A *true* hero. Blood sacrifice? The people understood the significance of something like that better than most of us do. This story was not familiar or comfortable in this setting. It demanded a response.

As we left, of course, I wanted to know the score. Had the people made professions of faith? Again Reverend Lodinyo smiled, now showing that same patience with me. "It doesn't work that way," he said. "Words alone will not generate belief. That's the work of the Holy Spirit."

He seemed patient and confident about his assertion. And sure enough, I was told that when the reverend returned several months later, there were small gatherings, "churches," that had set Reverend Lodinyo's message to their traditional melody and were singing it together.

The story of Jesus just *works*, no matter the culture. It's certainly not a tale any of us would manufacture for the purpose of selling to people. If we'd made it up, the hero wouldn't die. We wouldn't have witness testimony from the empty tomb given by women (in ancient culture, they weren't taken seriously and couldn't testify in court). The cross itself was the ultimate mark of shame in the Roman world, reserved for the worst criminals. Who would build a faith around the lowest mark of humiliation and pain?

Who would base the success of that new faith on eleven very sketchy characters, mostly fishermen and peasants, who had never ventured more than a few miles from home? Who would choose backwater Judea as a base? Or build on an ethic of turning the other cheek and denying self? Only the most inept marketers in the history of commerce would foist such a thing on the public. And the story is made even more amazing in that it toppled the greatest political empire in history and become the world's leading belief system.

Can I prove Jesus? No, but perhaps I would submit the above to the court of common sense. If His miracles and resurrection seem difficult to believe, how much less likely is the story after that—the story of exponential international spreading of the faith—which we *know* to be true? That's a lot of changed lives over two thousand years.

As I thought about this idea of proof—so important to the modern mind—I realized how many truly important things in life cannot be proven. Can you "prove" your love for your spouse or children? Can you quantify or measure happiness? Grief? Blaise Pascal said that "the heart has its reasons, which the reason cannot know." In other words, the heart ventures where scientists fear to tread.

When Kris, my wife, faced cancer, I spoke to some of the world's greatest medical minds at the Mayo Clinic. I made a point of asking each doctor if he or she believed in miracles. Invariably, they said yes. Some went on to explain that medical outcomes often violate the dictates of science, and the only explanation left standing is the miraculous. They'd witnessed such things time and time again.

My view of Jesus requires faith. But competing views would require more of it—for example, the belief that our universe came together through random circumstance, with no guiding mind, no designer, no purpose. The wonder of galaxies, the variety of the animal kingdom, the beauty of the color spectrum, and the depths of human emotions—all of these things without design, just happenstance?

The Greeks believed a god named Apollo pulled the sun across the sky in his chariot. Scientists have found instead that the sun is a ball of gas around which our world revolves. But have scientists therefore said all that can be said on the subject—or have they described the fingerprints of divine work?

Someone has to explain how something—a universe—can come out of nothing. Kai Nelson, former atheist and philosopher, offers an illustration. Suppose we hear a loud noise. *Bang!* You turn to me and ask, "What made that noise?"

I say, "Nothing. It just happened."

If you were sensible at all, you'd scoff. *Nothing* comes from nothing. The big bang theory carries that same looming question. The current consensus of the atheistic wing of science is that that bang came from nothing at all.

Most of us can grasp that principle. But over the last few decades, we've come to understand that it's only the beginning of the questions raised when one subtracts God from the creation of the universe. The universe isn't just *here*; it has been *fine-tuned*. Intelligent life isn't exactly a flexible proposition. The requirements for it are incredibly severe.

The great physicist Stephen Hawking tells us that if the rate of expansion of the universe one second after the big bang had been smaller by one part in a hundred thousand million, the universe would have collapsed back in upon itself, into a great fireball.

There are a great many measurements, from entropy to gravity to the speed of our planet's spin, that are intensively, precisely fine-tuned to allow organic life, particularly on our planet. Gravity couldn't be off, in either direction, by even an unthinkably tiny amount, or we wouldn't be here. Life could not be sustained.

When one measures the numbers and necessities that we now know must be present for the infinitesimally small chance of successful life, there is no particular reason for any of those requirements to have set in. Not in a random universe. Any one of them alone, by its absence, would have doomed any chance of life. Yet *every* one of them has been followed, right down the line, and here we are eating and breathing and thinking about it. More than that—we are emoting. We are experiencing joy and grief, creating art, composing symphonies. Pretty good for the random collections of molecules we're said to be.

Just think from an artistic perspective. The sun is four hundred times the diameter of the moon—but by "random happenstance," the moon is four hundred times closer. Thus, they appear to be the same relative size in the sky, they form a perfect eclipse, and we learn that the distance of the moon from us is another factor that is perfect for its effect on the tides and other things.

The sun, of course, is just the right distance for the climates we need. The moon is a stabilizing factor for the earth's axis of rotation. It's right where we need it.

Considering all these things, Nelson concludes that it's the theologian who has the true odds on his or her side, not the advocate of random, God-free chance.

I've read about a number of scientists who haven't abandoned faith because of their learning—and others who have concluded that some things simply can't be casually assigned to accident.

Then there's the moral issue, completely apart from physics. C. S. Lewis was a literary scholar, not a scientist. But his arguments for the existence of God in his book *Mere Christianity* were enough to convince Dr. Francis Collins, director of the National Human Genome Research Institute, from a commonsense view. It stood to reason that surely there had to be a creator. But a personal one? That was Collins' struggle.

In the end, Lewis' work won Collins over with its argument that there is moral law as well as physical. Why do we know what is right and what is wrong? People everywhere agree on the basic rules, such as the immorality of taking life. Why? Where does that come from?

Some atheists have argued that ideas of "right" and "wrong" are a matter of human evolution—something we find convenient for our societies. But that doesn't wash, because we so often find that the right thing to do isn't convenient at all!

Pure survival of the fittest would have us killing and stealing. Moral law doesn't fit in there at all. If our only drive is to preserve our DNA, why does one give his or her life for another? Why do we love sacrificially?

Our hearts, in other words, stubbornly insist on a God, and one who is good, who stands for certain ways and laws and principles that don't come easy to us at all. And we have a conscience that takes the side of this mysterious spiritual impulse rather than the supposedly powerful force of survival instinct.

In the end, the scientist and the believer need not fight. They're looking at the same subject matter through two different lenses (and it takes two lenses to make spectacles). The fact is that physical and spiritual investigations can and should have a friendly relationship.

I came to conclude that those without a belief in God are people of faith, just like me. They are banking on the fact that all the evidence pointing to God—physically and morally—is misdirected somehow. And with the question of what happens after death, they're doubling down on that conclusion. It's a high-stakes wager.

And what about me? If I die and turn out to be wrong, and death is truly death, then I'll have lost nothing but gained a life of tremendous joy and purpose (another "proof" of God, in my view).

Thus, I hope that, like those people in Africa, my atheistic friends have turned away yet still are hearing. Still listening. "Foolishness!" they may say for now. But as my missionary friend taught me, the story has power that words are insufficient to carry. This is why Simon Guillebaud writes in *Choose Life* that where words leave off, impotent to the nonbeliever, a changed life cannot be ignored. The Pharisees once badgered a young man, citing all the rules against healing on the Sabbath and all the "problems" about Jesus, and the young man responded, "Whether he is a sinner or not, I don't know. One thing I do know. I was blind but now I see" (John 9:25).

As time went on, I felt something like that young man. Philosophical debates may have been out of my depth at times. I couldn't answer for all the mysteries of faith or so-called biblical contradictions. I only knew that once I had been blind, but now I could see.

We're left with the mystery of coming to faith. It's not a mental exercise, a doctrinal checklist. It's ultimately simpler, something a child can do, without a philosopher anywhere in sight. Jesus described it in a word picture: "I stand at the door and knock" (Revelation 3:20). Whether to turn the knob and throw open the door is the most basic of decisions. And once I did so, everything changed for me.

Words and fine arguments—even some of these reflections on the universe and its design—have their place, but for the most part I find they don't change people. What does change them is the experience of seeing someone who was one person and now is entirely another. Where there was stress, there is now peace. Where there was restlessness, there is now purpose. Where there was grim resolve, there are now hope and joy and new energy.

We all understand that a zebra can't change its stripes. But God can.

5

Alone but Not Alone

Mr. Busy Pants Becomes a Hermit

◆━━◆

Be still, and know that I am God.
—Psalm 46:10

Our hearts are restless, until they can find rest in you.
—Saint Augustine

Death had stripped me of my father. Africa had stripped me of my self-concept. The future of my life was a blank sheet of paper—and I've never been one for empty agendas. My whole life consisted of to-do lists.

Even though I'd been humbled, even though I'd seen the limits of my personal world view, the great lessons don't take hold overnight. I still saw myself as a highly ambitious Type A overachiever, an aggressive business personality who would surely be one of the choicer weapons in heaven's arsenal.

Maybe it was something like that apostle Paul guy, and Africa was my road to Damascus. After all, Paul was a high achiever like me—a go-getter—and God had said, "I need this guy on my team! I'll just zap him and put him at the front of the line." So, I blush to admit that, as I returned home in 1993, I was a new man but still a little half-baked. More than I realized at the time, the jerk lived on.

What it really came down to what this: I had the right intentions and the right heart, but I didn't know Jesus. I only knew *about* Him.

I was who I was. I'd heard that sermon about Mary and Martha having Jesus over for dinner, how Martha raced through the house doing her chores as Mary sat at the Master's feet. I took Martha's side without having to think twice. Life is about getting things done. You go and do if you want to earn the right to sit and soak. Besides, I've always been more comfortable going and doing. Sitting and soaking makes me a little crazy.

It made perfect sense to me that God had plenty of Marys already. He needed a few more Marthas to keep the machinery running, and He'd chosen me. But the time came when somehow the truth broke through even the thickness of my head, and I realized the presumption of believing God needed me to do anything at all. Or believing He needed me, period. In a rare moment of lucidity, I realized He must be having a good laugh over my sense of personal value and self-importance.

God doesn't need me and most likely doesn't need you either. That's what makes Him God, if you'll overlook the foggy theology.

To put it another way, it's the perennial birthday question. What do you give the God who has everything? In my wiser moments, as one more layer of the old foolish Ward Brehm was peeled away, I came up with an answer to that question. There *was* something I could give Him.

The gift was so stunningly simple. *Presence.* (No, not *presents.*) I needed to be there wholly for Him. All my time, all my attention, all my devotion. I could understand this, because my own father's presence had always meant more than any presents he could give me. He made himself completely available to me. And if my heavenly Father did the same, how else could I respond?

That was going to mean some sitting and soaking, unfortunately. And part of me already began to protest. *Any alternatives, Lord? You know I'm not the type. Just wondering if there's a plan B for us Type As.*

But I already knew the answer. I needed to make the arrangements to be alone, one-on-one, God and me.

I'd heard somewhere about a silent retreat called Pacem in Terris (which translates to "peace on earth"). Just to hear the words is to begin to feel a little of that rest and solitude. The retreat is about an hour and a half north of Minneapolis, near the town of Isanti, Minnesota. Soon, I found the Pacem in Terris website and was seeing pictures of immense natural beauty—something out of Tolkien, almost. There were individual dwellings called hermitages. The founder, Shirley Wanchena, had heard the directive of God to create an environment where his people can come and be alone with Him.

I made the call and actually spoke to an angel. That's how I felt at the time, and I'm pretty sure I had it right, as you'll see.

"Hello, this is Ward Brehm," I said. "I'm calling from Minneapolis, and I'm interested in staying in a hermitage next week."

"That would be wonderful!"

"Now, I've read up on the Web, and I see where you recommend a stay of at least two nights. The thing is, I'm only available for one."

"That's okay. We're just happy you called, and we're already looking forward to having you with us."

Over the next few days, I mentioned my plans to a few close friends. Then I did what it's in my nature to do: I loaded a briefcase and an additional satchel with all my spiritual readings and a library of to-do lists that I fully intended to plow through during my stay.

One of my closest brothers, Steve Moore—whose daily e-mail posting, "Scripture of the Day" feature, is now read by thousands—wanted me to know he was already praying for me and that he had one small word of advice. "Ward," he said. "I know you, and I'm going to urge you take nothing but your Bible. Leave the other stuff behind."

Oh, but he didn't understand. I had a full agenda, plenty to do, but it was all about Jesus. I'd be busy, but I'd be Jesus-busy, and I would get every bit of it done as sure as I was Ward Brehm. Which I was, which was the problem.

As I drove onto the grounds of Pacem in Terris, the natural beauty and solitude impressed me deeply. I felt I was on holy ground. I parked my car and entered the main lodge, and there was my angel, Shirley, the founder of Pacem in Terris. Over the phone, I'd been impressed with her gentle demeanor and kindness. In person, I knew I'd had it right when I thought of her as a messenger from heaven. She went through all the logistics and shared a bit of the place's history, but it wasn't the spiel you'd get from a forest ranger or camp director. This was someone who knew about the power of time with God. It emanated from her.

"How can we pray for you during your stay?" she asked.

"We?"

"Yes. You'll be staying in Saint Anthony's hermitage. Approximately 125 former occupants of that lodge have made a covenant to lift you up in prayer while you're here."

"Really?" I had never heard of such a thing, and I felt a deep tug of emotion.

"Really. Many past hermits have come to this place, then agreed to 'pray it forward' for others who follow them. I have only one additional piece of advice."

I had a slight sense of déjà vu. Did hermitages recognize déjà vu?

"When you go through the gates of silence," she said, "bring only your Bible."

I could ignore the instruction once, but now, in the presence of this woman of God, I knew I was at checkmate. In my mind's eye, I saw all my agendas and lists and well-laid plans slipping away from me. "Okay," I said. And now it was on. I was going to go crazy with withdrawal pangs from my addiction of choice: details.

I might have grumbled to myself, but only a little. I made my way up the well-kept footpath to my hermitage and opened the door to a beautifully unadorned, unembellished one-room dwelling. The key feature of the room was a pane of glass—a floor-to-ceiling picture window overlooking a spectacular forest. So even indoors, one was surrounded by the magnificence of God's creation.

I looked over my surroundings, put away the few things I had, and wasn't quite sure what to do with myself. I could almost hear the loaded briefcase and extra satchel calling to me from back in my car, but I did my best to put these things out of my mind. I was alone, and that was the point. Paper is just a substitute for people or anything else we use to feel the void.

This was all about clearing away every little thing that might block out the voice of God, and it was time to face that squarely.

I sat down, looked at my hands, and had my first difficult question: *Why?* Why is solitude so terrifying to someone like me? How is it that busyness becomes a refuge in which to hide, even for a lifetime? And what exactly was I hiding from?

I thought about the city and the people I knew, so many of them just as driven and just as allergic to the silence—a whole world of refugees from reflection and serious self-examination. No wonder so many of us are burned out, confused, and desperately chasing every kind of escape. There's a great hole inside us we won't acknowledge. We step around that hole as we go about our work. We dress it up with accomplishments and success and even charitable works. We pretend the hole isn't there. But every now and then we find ourselves gazing into its depths, and we feel the emptiness.

The French mathematician and philosopher Blaise Pascal once wrote in his famous *Pensées* that he believed all the unhappiness of humanity comes from not knowing how to sit quietly in a room. This, he said, is why we give our freedom to hustle and bustle, and use a prison cell as the gravest punishment. We have no idea how to experience the pleasures of solitude.

But this thing I was facing wasn't mere solitude, was it? The whole point of it was that I was alone but not alone. I was in the presence of God. And this added a separate layer of anxiety. What could I do with that? I knew, like most Christians, how to talk about God. I could speak in the vague terms of "a personal relationship with Jesus," but if I possessed such a thing, wouldn't we be holding conversations? Wouldn't I have an intense sense of His presence?

What if I talked to God and He didn't talk back? What then?

I was having the feelings and asking the questions, I'm sure, that everyone must face. It's the anxiety of moving to a deeper and less certain stage of holy engagement. It's the point in time when you've been a child and become quite comfortable on the shallow end of the pool, but some friend has beckoned you toward the deep end. What will you do when your feet no longer feel the floor? What if you go under? What if, in fact, you can't swim?

I had always thought of the concept of aloneness with God as something comforting and nice. Getting serious about it was not comforting at all. It was frightening. It challenged me to the very core of who I was. It stripped away all the masks and pretenses by which I lived and forced me to be honest with myself. For, though I may not have realized it, God was already in that room. He was already working on me. We tend to wait for some inner sensation, some acute feeling of His presence, but only in retrospect do we often find His fingerprints on our thoughts and emotions and realizations.

Not knowing what else to do, I prayed my own version of David's "Search me, God" prayer in Psalm 139 and told the Lord that this time was His and no one and nothing else's, that I was a fumbling, stumbling believer, but I wanted to know His presence. I surrendered my time and myself.

Shirley had told me that she sees many "hermits" who are clearly tired but don't realize it. She said she'd be praying for my rest. Well, that wasn't a problem for me—not a guy with my level of energy. It was still early afternoon, and I didn't feel the least bit tired. All systems were go. As a matter of fact, I wouldn't mind a brisk hike through those woods. And with that thought, I stretched out on the little bed and fell into a deep sleep for three hours.

I awoke and wondered, *How did that happen?* I thought again about that brisk hike, and decided to investigate one of the many enticing trails that run through the hermitage, twist on through the forest, and wrap themselves around gorgeous fields of wild flowers. I began to walk and found myself wondering what was wrong with my ears—it was far too quiet. Shouldn't there be birds, crickets, soft breezes rattling the branches? It felt as if God had hit the mute button on the world of nature.

What I was missing was conversation, even the one with my own inner voice, who was constantly planning, calculating, bullet-pointing my procession through life. My briefcase and satchel, I realized, had stopped calling out to me from inside the car. Perhaps they'd found something else to do.

I was starting to get it. This was a *retreat*. I was now at a safe distance from all those things. There was God and there was me, and this was our time.

As the path carried me into a clearing, I was stunned to see a very old, weather-beaten handcrafted cross. It looked so beautiful, so natural even as a manmade thing. I walked up to it very closely and felt the tears begin to well in my eyes. Something about that cross, there in the midst of the deep forest, symbolized the insistent presence of God in the thickness and deep overgrowth of my life.

I walked on, now thinking and reflecting as if it were the most natural thing in the world for me. Being totally exposed to God, without reservation, without a safety net, is a terrifying proposition. It's locking the door to one's comfort zone and walking far away from it. From there, you can look back and get a view of your life that would be available no other way. I saw the details and initiatives and activities of my life for what they really were—nice, comfortable tools, but no replacement for an inner life. None of it made any kind of gift to God.

What I could give Him, however, was my presence. I could offer Him my soul with all the adornments stripped away. I wanted my life to be like my hermitage—a simple and sincere construction with one great window that reflected the reality of God. Anything else was like trying to use cheap furniture and a coat of paint to compete with that view of the forest that came through the glass. God wanted me as an empty room, one He could fill with light.

As Shirley must have suspected, I was bound to return, and for more than one night. So far, I've never made it more than two consecutive nights, but I've found that it takes a day just to decompress, air out the mind, and throw open the doors to the heart. My goal is to stay a week at Pacem in Terris. And as much as I'd love to tell you that it becomes easy, that you can become a ninja hermit, I haven't found that to be true. I'm still addicted to the circus of modern life. I still revert back to my default, which is made of lists and agendas and sticky-note reminders. I keep thinking they'll make me feel important, which is why I need to return again and again to the place where I discover what really does matter.

Just as it's all too easy to import my briefcase mentality to the retreat, I long for a day when I can export the retreat to the world of my briefcase, when I can walk through the city with the same awareness of God that I find in that forest. I do realize that no one place has an exclusive contract on His presence—even Pacem in Terris. Psalm 139, which I paraphrased in my prayer that first night in my hermitage, goes on to remind us that God's presence truly is everywhere:

Where can I go from your Spirit?
Where can I flee from your presence?
If I go up to the heavens, you are there;

if I make my bed in the depths, you are there.
If I rise on the wings of the dawn,
if I settle on the far side of the sea,
even there your hand will guide me,
your right hand will hold me fast. (Psalm 139:7–10)

Yes, that's what I want: the will to give God my presence so I can feel His presence—wherever I go. But Pacem in Terris will always be holy ground for me. As I wrote this chapter and reflected upon my encounters with God in that place, I received an e-mail from Father Tim, who serves there now:

> *It was about a year ago this time that you and Kris came to visit Shirley in her declining days. You were among the last folks she asked to see, outside of family, before her death. After you left, I'll never forget: She called me in and said, "Put a special bench for Ward out under that big tree in the prairie."*
>
> *You'll be happy to know that bench is now in place, just as you and Shirley once imagined it together. Attached is a picture of it—a special place of peace and silence quietly waiting for you. We look forward to your next visit.*

The plan is to take God with me wherever I go. But I also believe that it's imperative for me to find the occasional time and place for a rendezvous with Jesus. He wants that more than anything I might be able to do on His behalf.

◀━▶

Alone but Not Alone

A place of great peace; a cathedral of stillness.
My window frames a stillborn painting of a forest at perfect rest.
Absolute silence. As if inside a deep bank vault. Or tomb.

A sanctuary from a life whirling, and of pointless egocentric driving.
Here accomplishments can be seen as they are:
fleeting wisps of smoke,
A refuge for ancient truths that,
although they come quiet as a whisper,
can at last be heard.

Alone but not Alone.

A safe harbor filled with promise of new beginnings
and great hope.
Yet the thought of being alone and fully exposed
to the constant gaze of almighty God
is as uncomfortable as it is reassuring.
The late November sun surrenders early to the winter solstice.
Forest resplendent with spectacular streaks of sunset
until gray fades to darkness …
then to a moonlit tapestry of frozen shadows.
And a sleep without dreams.

Alone but not Alone.

The morning brings promise of everything new.
And an overwhelming sense of gratitude to be on this road.
The adventure of a lifetime … searching for my soul.
Praying for new beginnings.
Wanting to lose myself. To use the multitude
of blessings given to me. To serve.
I am in quest of the Shepherd so far in the distance
who calls … but with the noise of a busy life, I often cannot hear.

Alone but not Alone.

The narrow path through frozen trees that have
forsaken their leaves,
standing naked and still. Exposed. Like me.

Winding down to a small pond surrounded by marsh.
Yesterday alive with flocks of noisy ducks and geese
sounding alarm at my intrusion.
This morning dead silent ... covered with a blanket of ice.
The busyness over. The lake preparing for a deep and long sleep.
In not so long my life, too, will have its own frozen cover
and I shiver briefly
with both a calm fear and confident anticipation
from that small glimpse into eternity.

Alone but not Alone.

The well-worn footpath emerges from forest to prairie.
My gaze locks on an old roughhewed cross in the clearing.
Standing meek and inconspicuous
yet holding incomprehensible authority.
My knees are sore and fingers frozen when I finally rise,
but my soul is song of the promise of sins
both forgiven and forgotten.
At great cost, my guilt taken away and burden shared.
Facing both the hope and challenge of trying
to forsake myself and ways familiar,
and instead, follow a bit more closely this strange
and compelling Shepherd of souls.[1]

6

Two-Minute Warning

The Mystery of Prayer

To have God speak to the heart is a majestic experience,
an experience that people may miss if they monopolize the
conversation and never pause to hear God's responses.

—CHARLES STANLEY

Doug Coe, from Washington, DC, both a good friend and mentor, recently died after leading a life totally devoted to following Jesus. He always challenged and encouraged me at the same time. Quite a gift! His passing leaves a huge hole in my life.

Not too many years ago during a long talk, Doug startled me with this statement: "Brother, your problem is you don't pray enough."

"What are you talking about?" I asked, no doubt indignantly. "You can't possibly know how much or how little I pray."

"I can just tell." He smiled. "Are you telling me you do pray enough?"

"Well … no." Touché.

"I thought not. And since we were talking about spiritual growth—you don't read Scripture enough either."

I opened my mouth, then shut it quickly. I wasn't about to challenge him a second time.

He then related a story about a speaking engagement where he addressed the Young Presidents' Organization, a group of powerful CEOs under forty. At the end of his talk to them, he offered a wager. "I'd guess we have fifty 'rich young rulers' in this room," he said. "I'll bet each of you one thousand dollars. All you have to do is pray for two minutes on your knees, and read the Gospels plus Acts for five minutes each day, for six weeks—and my bet is that God will change your life forever."

These young CEOs were intrigued; they liked challenges. Forty-five days later, checks began to roll in from men who knew they'd lost the wager. The checks were accompanied by some pretty amazing stories. There was not a single note from anyone claiming they had won the bet, but one note that came in simply said, *God didn't do anything—but the experience itself has changed me. Attached is my $1,000.*

It was a good story. "Cool," I said, still rattled a bit by his observations about my prayer and Bible study status. And why was he telling me this story?

"Well, what do you think?" he asked. "Will you take the bet?"
Uh-oh.

But I was as much of a sucker as those business people. The wheels were turning in my mind. Two minutes of prayer? Five minutes of reading? Seven minutes out of twenty-four hours. Piece of cake, even for a busy, driven guy like me. "Deal," I said, and we shook on it.

Doug saw my confident smile, and he began to grin as well. "It's harder than you think," he said. "Especially the prayer part."

"What, two minutes?" I gave him my most skeptical look.

"Will you commit to using a stopwatch? And you'll be on your knees?"

"You're kidding, right?"

"I'm completely serious. Like the business of really praying is. All sorts of crazy things are going to come into your mind while you're praying. It's an obstacle course of distractions, brother. But you've got to focus for two minutes. Being on your knees helps.

Knowing your time frame does too. Just let the thoughts flow. Give them to God and keep on praying. Two minutes—on your knees—with a stopwatch."

Doug has a way of enticing you toward a spiritual goal. And I figured he was onto something. I know my faith in God is deep and sincere, but I'm not at all consistent with prayer. There are too many days when I pray over a meal, and that's all I have to say directly to God that day. What would happen if I was deliberate about prayer every day, as Doug challenged me to be?

Later that night, as I was preparing for bed, I realized I was just about to forget my commitment on the very first day! Not too promising a start. I changed directions, headed for my home office, and self-consciously fell to my knees to begin praying.

Doug was right. Suddenly my mind was a circus of distractions—crazy stuff, irrelevant stuff, anything to block the dialogue between God and me. When I'm working, that doesn't happen. I have a tight focus on whatever I'm doing, and it has allowed me to be successful in business. Where was that focus now?

I appreciated Doug's warning and decided I wasn't going to be defeated. I redoubled my efforts to pray clearly and with substance. The safari going on in my head began to abate, and I was able to focus more clearly. When I was certain I'd passed the two-minute mark, I pulled myself to my feet and glanced at my watch.

Forty-five seconds. Oops.

Totally humbled, I finished my prayer, making sure I put in all 120 seconds—talk about a two-minute warning—and then I turned to my Bible. I found that considerably easier. As a matter of fact, I didn't want to stop at five minutes. Where did the time go? As time went on, I read well into the book of Matthew.

I wasn't thinking so much about the wager anymore. I was enjoying the spiritual discipline of things.

Forty days came and went, and I never missed a session. I was more than a little proud of myself, and when I realized *that*, I was more than a little ashamed of myself. I wasn't supposed to be doing this for pride. Seven minutes a day devoted to the Creator of the universe didn't qualify me as a spiritual giant. I have many friends who pray with their face to the floor for hours on end. I also have friends who have read through the Bible multiple times and can actually quote plenty of what they read.

I'd certainly read in the Gospels what Jesus had to say about prayer. He told us not to be like the hypocrites, who love giving lofty prayers on the street corners and in the synagogues, anywhere they know they'll be seen. Jesus says that if what they want is acclaim, they've got their full reward. The rest of us should want a greater reward, and we get it when we pray in secret (Matthew 6:5–6).

Jesus went on to teach His disciples a prayer that lasts not two minutes, not one minute—but a quarter of a minute. The Lord's Prayer, as He taught it, is quite short—and I was surprised to learn that the part beginning "thine is the kingdom" wasn't part of the original. That's part of a benediction added by the early church, though it's a good one. My point is, Jesus had no problem with a brief prayer. What He wanted was one from the heart. I'll admit to growing impatient with those public prayers that drone on like State of the Union addresses, pickled with opinions and important announcements. Those "prayers" work out more as earthbound speeches than heaven-bound pleas, and I think about those warnings concerning hypocrites and Pharisees.

While Doug and I had our wager, there were no discernible miracles in my life. I didn't hit the lottery. Nobody in my family was miraculously cured—that would come later. It turned out that the thing Jesus did was embedded in the wager itself—as I learned to pray with focus and to embrace the serious study of Scripture, the discipline of my spiritual life deepened. And of course, that had a profound effect on everything else. I had to admit that, if it was a kind of sucker bet, Doug won it. As long as you keep the conditions he sets out, truly praying and truly studying Scripture, he can't help but win. The thing is, so do you. Everybody wins, which makes it a unique wager.

As time went on, and I was more thoughtful about the place of prayer, life began to bring me new insights from various quarters. One of these came from my friends in Ethiopia, one of the African nations I visited.

I was in a remote village in Antsokia Valley. We had arrived for our visit, and we were told there were pastors who had walked up to fifty kilometers (more than thirty miles) to meet with us. But we were several hours late, and it was after dark by the time we entered the ancient monastery where they awaited us. They sat there in the dark, preserving the kerosene that would have lit their lanterns. But as they heard us coming, the lanterns gave their light, and it was a picturesque scene—like going back in time.

The flickering light made the shadows dance. The voices were quiet and the spirits were eager. We were told that the men had prayed for us *all night long* the previous evening, as we were traveling from Addis Ababa. In the dark, I heard the voice of my friend Bill Bieber. "Ward," he whispered, "are we in that much danger?" These men had walked for many hours, waited in darkness, prayed in faith, and covered us in love. It was incredibly humbling.

Someone in our group asked, "How is it even possible to pray all night long?"

The men whispered a bit, and a few shreds of light revealed shy smiles. The elder pastor said, "When we pray, mostly we listen to what Jesus is telling us." He paused, then added, "When you Americans pray, it often seems as you do all of the talking."

Silence.

He was so very right, of course.

Prayer is a commodity we've devalued in our culture, an opportunity for lip service, as Jesus suggested from the very beginning. How often does a friend share a deep burden of his heart, and I tell him he'll be in my thoughts and prayers—only to forget the whole thing within an hour or two? To my shame, I must admit I've done it too many times.

I once asked my pastor and spiritual mentor, Dr. Arthur Rouner, how he handles so many people asking for his prayer. He told me something very wise: he refuses to make promises difficult to keep. Instead of promising a prayer at some time in the future, he seizes the fact that there's no time like the present. "Let's pray about it right now," he'll say, whether on the phone or in person. Then he writes down the name. As he was telling me about this, he pulled the day's sheet out of his breast pocket wallet—a crumpled, worn slip of paper with scrawled names all over it. "I carry them next to my heart, wherever I go," he said.

As an immature believer, most of my prayers were Santa Claus–level: "Give me this, and this, and this." I had a list in my head of requests. Sometimes we get that idea about prayer, because at church and other gatherings, we offer prayer requests that way—our requests are simply lists of illnesses and job needs and the like. It's easy to view God as an ATM, but I'm fairly confident God longs for much deeper conversation.

I have tried my best to move beyond the superficiality of those kinds of prayers and understand better that prayer is meant to be a much more mysterious thing. When Kris was diagnosed with terminal cancer, for example, we prayed without ceasing that God would perform a miracle and save her life. We learned all about desperate, emotional, focused prayer that comes when God is our only refuge.

The mystery comes in the question of why He said yes to that one and may say no to the next one. Two of my closest friends lost their young and beautiful wives to a similar form of cancer. What do you say to comfort people in such times? And just when Kris was pronounced free of cancer by the Mayo Clinic five years subsequent to her miracle, her youngest sister, Karla, was diagnosed with a similar form of ovarian cancer. Karla died six months later, leaving her two sons without a mother. My close friend Steve, who is a devoted follower of Jesus, lost Lori, his wife, shortly after Kris was cured. Huge and unanswerable questions.

I know there must be people who observe such things and believe God is cruel, random, or simply absent—or maybe He plays favorites. I don't think any of these charges are true. I can't answer the tough questions, but I do have my own approaches to prayer.

For example, I try hard not to pray for outcomes. For me, to say, "Give me this, Lord," implies that I have a better idea of what is wise and right than He does. Real faith is trusting Him with those outcomes. I try to make fewer demands and more professions of love for Jesus. I pray for His kingdom to come and His will to be done and ask Him to align me with those goals however it pleases Him to do so. My prayer is designed to help me say, "Lord, whatever it is you do in this world, I trust it. I accept it in advance, and will love you unconditionally, just as you have loved me unconditionally." I love Him not for what He will do for me, but for who He is.

And prayer helps me understand that God's sovereignty is beyond my understanding. It helps me accept and embrace the mystery. God never promised to remove our enemies. In Psalm 23, He promises to prepare a table for us *in the presence* of our enemies. He doesn't promise to show us a detour through the valley of the shadow—He promises to walk through it with us.

Prayer for me is also about gratitude, which changes my outlook on everything. I remember all that God has done, even in the space of a simple day, and I'm overwhelmed by the extraordinary blessings He has given me. I feel true hope.

As I understand the Scriptures, God knows what we need even before we ask it. So why should I behave as if I'm giving Him the news for the first time?

"I need this and this and this, Lord."

"Yes, I know. I *always* know."

Thinking this through, my organized, straight-to-business personality inspires me to suggest: Why not cut the list out entirely, cut right to the chase, and be still and ask God to give *me* the list?

Now there's a thought. I think of Arthur Rouner with that wonderful list of names close to his heart, and I imagine him meeting with God. I wonder if God says, "Now, let me give you the names close to *my* heart." And there might be names we'd never have thought about—people who are not the "squeaky wheels who get all the grease," people quietly in need of encouragement. Perhaps then I would not only pray for them but go to them and serve them.

I recall when I was reading Psalms and came across this verse: "Take delight in the LORD, and he will give you the desires of your heart" (Psalm 37:4). What a promise. All I had to do was be delighted with God and he would give me anything I wanted!

When I took this to my mentor in Scripture, Monty Sholund, he gently rebuked me. "That's not exactly what the verse means, Ward. What it really implies is that if you love the Lord with all your heart, He will give you *new* desires more in keeping with *His* will."

I imagine scenarios like that all the time, because it helps me in prayer—Jesus sitting in the chair across from me, smiling, eager for our time together, maybe saying, "You know what, Ward? I bet we could talk for even more than two minutes. I've seen you do it with other people." And we'd both laugh.

Prayer is one of the things that matters most, but it's a mystery to me. And I believe the moment it becomes anything less, I've lost something valuable. The late Henri Nouwen, who sailed in some deep waters spiritually, called on us to be mystics as we approach the love of God. That's a very literal understanding of what it means to dwell in the presence of an invisible God. The discipline of contemplative prayer is the insistence of departing from the tyranny of the urgent, from the stress of the here and now, and entering a spiritual reality that we can't see and sometimes can't feel—but that we trust in faith. It anchors us in the love of God. It reaffirms the real truth about us, the truth the world tries to contradict—that we belong to God, that the world itself belongs to him, and that what seems vast and important is only vaporous and fading.

Monty also helped me understand prayer. I told him I was praying for a friend who was recently diagnosed with cancer, and he turned to me and said, "Ward, it's very important that you understand that prayer doesn't work."

At first I was shocked and quickly grew indignant. What kind of thing was that to say? If it was a joke, it was in extremely poor taste, considering my friend's terrible prognosis. How could he say it didn't work? But he was dead serious. "Prayer doesn't work," he said, looking me squarely in the eye. Then, with a bit of a twinkle in his own, he added, "God works!"

I had to think about this. But Monty wasn't playing with words. There's an immense difference in using a formula and trusting God. I don't use prayer to get things; I use it to know God more intimately. And that's what I'm really trying to do more of.

I recently attended a guided retreat at a Catholic monastery, and the wise old priest guiding us gave a very simple but powerful formula for praying. He encouraged us to simply break our prayers into these four segments:

- I love you, Jesus (worship).
- I'm sorry, Jesus (confession).
- I need you, Jesus (requests).
- Thank you, Jesus (thanksgiving).

I have found praying this way most helpful. It keeps me focused on the fundamentals and hopefully also consistent with the Lord's Prayer that Jesus taught us to pray.

I'm beginning to realize that prayer isn't an obligation but a tremendous privilege. When I consider that I can sit in my home and have a conversation with the Creator of the universe, the King of all kings, at any time and without protocol or special requirements of any kind—without using anything other than my mind and my will—it's a huge change in perspective. My goal is to realize how much God yearns for those conversations with me and to find myself yearning more for them.

I close these thoughts with one of my favorite Benedictine prayers:

> May God bless you with a restless discomfort
> about easy answers, half-truths, and superficial relationships,
> so that you may seek truth boldly and love deep within your heart.
>
> May God bless you with holy anger at injustice, oppression,
> and exploitation of people, so that you may tirelessly work for
> justice, freedom, and peace among all people.
>
> May God bless you with the gift of tears
> to shed with those who suffer
> from pain, rejection, starvation, or the loss
> of all that they cherish, so that you may
> reach out your hand to comfort them
> and transform their pain into joy.
>
> May God bless you with enough foolishness to believe that
> you really can make a difference in this world, so that you are able,
> with God's grace, to do what others claim cannot be done.[1]

Let it be so.

7

Airplane Mode

Shedding Light on Going Dark

Slow down, you move too fast,
Got to make the morning last.

—Paul Simon, "The 59th Street Bridge Song"

Keen observation of the rat race reveals
that even if you win, you are still a rat.

—Lily Tomlin

I had no chance of leaving Africa in the dust of my frantic life path. The experience had cut too deeply. This was a relationship that would build, and I would be returning. I always knew that.

But *fifty* plus returns?

Over the years, I'd approach that milestone. The more I visited Africa, the more I found that needed to be done. But going there was something for me too. Each trip was a unique event, each one transformational in some way. I found that if God seemed to have fallen silent in my life, I knew where to go to catch up with Him.

One recent excursion took me to the Democratic Republic of the Congo via Rwanda. The trip would consume only a week, even with the traveling required. Generally, it takes so long to get there and to return, you plan on staying a while. But I'm no sightseer at this point; I tend to return to the continent with a more defined purpose.

This trip was all about Asili, our social-enterprise zone innovation. Asili is a market-based model that allows community members to purchase basic healthcare and clean drinking water, and help with agricultural techniques. After it was opened, the Asili health clinic was seeing hundreds of patients and working toward a special goal of reducing mortality for children under five. On this trip I brought along a group of potential donors and investors.

I wanted my friends to see what was possible, to be as excited as I was, and to commit to partnering in Asili's future. But as I prepared to travel, I thought once again of the old three-week trips—journeys just a bit more like the explorers took, before computers and iPads and cell phones. Then, you really had a feeling of slipping off the edge of the world (at least the Western world) and being out of touch. When David Livingstone was beating a path through the heart of the continent, he could have been anywhere within thousands of miles; no one could even be sure he was alive.

Not so much these days. By the time I embarked on this trip, phone and Internet were available at many points. Modern conveniences could be enjoyed in African cities there just as they were in American cities. But by this time, I'd come to see the wisdom of a "no news is good news" policy. Let's say one of us told his wife he'd call on a regular basis, then encountered a lack of service for whatever reason. This would cause needless worry at home. So, we made it clear we were "going dark," and people shouldn't expect to hear from us except in the case of an emergency. It was wise from a practical standpoint, but I had other reasons for shutting down the telecommunications fix.

I had been shocked by the effect of unplugging. We were severing all connections to the daily rat race. No agenda but here and now—what our eyes could see and our ears could hear. No e-mail, texts, or updates from the office. Going off the grid turned out to be easier than anyone expected—it was a liberation of the mind and spirit. I watched the tension melt away from my friends and saw how it opened them completely to the miracles God was doing.

My breakthrough had come on an earlier another trip, in the midst of a lot of personal stress. This had to do with one of my companies. In the days leading up to my trip to East Africa, I wasn't sleeping much. I would give up, push the blankets and sheets aside, grab a cup of coffee, and drive in to the office long before dawn. By the time I came home, I was meeting the sun going the other way, and still tensed up.

Ten days into East Africa, I suddenly realized the difference in myself. It wasn't that I was feeling no anxiety over the big, bad business situation; I was feeling nothing else about it either. Other things loomed larger. And I'm not telling you the business issues at home were actually no big deal. These were significant problems, but on the continent of Africa, I was significantly engaged in the problems of others. Here were people around me with issues of food and clean water and health and mortality.

I took a minute and attempted to revisit the business issues, with the Atlantic Ocean between us, and found it all a bit hazy. By the standards of that world, it was important enough; by the standards of this one, well, no. I was caught up in the moment with my travel mates. And with God.

Now, on this trip to Rwanda, my friend Rich and I agreed to "go dark"—full airplane mode, just like those first trips. To ensure compliance, we made a wager large enough to create a big "ouch" if either of us were to sign on. It was a really hard decision for both of us. I'm not exactly sure why. These devices tether us to anxiety and angst—and make us think we're liking it. We end up embracing our phones as if they were our closest and truest friends. You'd think giving up our phone and Internet connection would be freeing, but instead it caused uncertainty and angst. Signs of addiction perhaps?

Phones and e-mail—those things were made to serve us, right?

We thought they were making our lives easier. In reality, they get the whip hand. My phone feeds my addiction to plans and details, to staying busy. Walking through the airport, I often catch myself frantically patting the pockets in my coat and pants for that reassuring little box, my smartphone. Yes, it's a "smart" phone if it can hoodwink me into thinking I'm the one calling the shots.

The phone needs constant attention, like a spoiled child. Sometimes I'm talking to someone, and my thoughts keep deflecting back to the phone. Do I have any new texts? E-mail? I'm distracted from people and places right in front of my nose because of a piece of plastic with a microchip. Even when I go to sleep, my phone won't tolerate being in another room. It wants to be within arm's reach.

There's no doubt the development of the smartphone was the big game changer of the last decade or so. I doubt we ever anticipated how it would change our lives. When the iPhone came out, they actually called it the Jesus phone, an irreverent reference to the Second Coming. That's because it's more than a phone. It's many thousands of times more powerful than the computer that sent the first man to the moon, *millions* of times cheaper, and a whole heck of a lot smaller. And almost every one of us has one.

Upon landing in Amsterdam on our way to Africa, Rich and I flipped the little switch on our iPhones to airplane mode, turned them off, and stored them in the back of our backpacks, not to be seen for ten days. Among many other things, I had time to think that week about this rat race that the little phone seems to thrive on. If I'm honest, I have to admit the problem isn't in Silicon Valley in some mad scientist's laboratory. The problem isn't even the rat race itself. The issue is how willing *I* am to run in the rat race. The phones are only catering to an addiction I've had since long before they were around.

I'm a doer, a problem solver. I see a business issue, a family issue, an issue of any kind at all, and I jump in, because I'm wired to do so. Sometimes I don't even look before I leap. I don't reflect on the wisest course of action. Busyness is who I am, and I wear my identity like a medal.

Richard Swensen is an author and doctor who has written a number of valuable books, including *Margin*, a book about restoring lost time to overloaded lives. He has also written a short reflection in his collection of devotionals, *A Minute of Margin*, in which he suggests that we're "breaking the speed limit of life." He writes that the speed with which we live is even in our vocabulary:

> We are a nation on the move and in a hurry, the people of the forward stampede. We eat fast food during rush hour. We ship by FedEx, place calls through Sprint, balance books on Quicken, and diet with SlimFast. We're hyper-living, like field mice on amphetamines at harvest time, moving so fast we're passing up photons.[1]

As I was rethinking my life and my priorities during this time in airplane mode, I returned to this idea of the rat race. At one point, I decided to try an experiment the next time I ran into a certain friend.

"Hey, how are ya, man?" I smiled, clapping him on the back.

"Great! How 'bout you?"

"Great, great ... couldn't be any finer! How is everything? Are you good? Family okay?"

"Oh yeah! Amazing! Yours?"

"Everybody's fine. How about *you*?"

It went on like this. You know us guys. Everything and everybody, just great! It was an "everything's great" standoff. Or maybe we should call it a bland-off. But here's what broke it. He got to the part that went, "So, you pretty busy?"

I paused just a beat and looked him in the eye. "Nope."

He stepped back, startled. I'd gone off script! Why, a guy wouldn't say this unless there was something major, maybe a terminal illness. "Oh ... really?" he said. "Are you okay?"

Well, I'd told him already that I was *great*. But I guess he wasn't listening the first time. "Actually, I'm better than okay. It's all good."

"But—I guess—business is just off, eh?"

"Oh, no, not at all. Business is cruising along at high altitude. But you asked if I was busy, and no, I'm not busy these days, to tell the truth. Maybe that's why it's all good." I doubled down on my grin.

My friend looked me over as if I were some visitor from a nearby galaxy, then said, "Well ... um, gotta be going, ya know? See ya!" And he nearly tripped over his two feet transporting himself to a new location.

I realized that we've made *busy* into something more than a badge of honor. It's our creed, our justification for existence. It violates the unwritten social code to say you're not busy. So even if you do have time on your hands, you never, ever *admit* such a thing. You don't want to create a scandal, do you?

I also realized that paying homage to the busy life, as we interact with each other, does bad things. It underlines, highlights, adorns, reaffirms, and enshrines the value that we need to keep churning, keep busy at all times. It has been said that the business of America is business itself, and I would change one letter to make it *busyness*.

Busyness, I believe, is greed. By filling my life with events, activities, and responsibilities that far exceed the boundaries God has set for humans to function well, I'm being greedy—greedy for experiences and accomplishments that are unrealistic, greedy for pleasing others and being acknowledged.

In a very real sense, I'm trying to escape my own mortality by trying to do more than God intended for me. Our culture constantly encourages us to lead lives of excess, assuring us that few things are beyond our reach if we only work hard enough and push the boundaries of human capability. This approach has infiltrated our lives, to the destruction of many of us. We simply cannot do and be everything we want, even if the goals are all good things.

Kris noticed how I was pushing the boundaries of busy: I was *multitasking*. That word didn't exist before 1965, and it was a *computer* word. We wanted computers that could do more than one thing at once—again, in the quest of making our lives simpler. Instead, we've appropriated that word into human behavior, so that we've made our lives more complex. We're trying to become computers.

Kris saw my version of this as we were driving along in the car. I glanced over and saw she was staring at me with a mix of odd fascination and outright horror. I was steering the car, talking on the phone, and changing the radio station all at the same time. She wouldn't have been too surprised if I'd grown a third arm at some point—then I wouldn't have to steer with my knees.

Keeping busy, I had long accepted, was a status symbol. It convinced others—and me—that I was successful. Africa unraveled all my assumptions and forced me to revisit that idea. Soon I began to see that success has nothing to do with activity. As I define it, genuine success has a lot more to do with *the quality of being fully present in the moment*.

The more of ourselves we give to right here and right now, the more fully we are living. It's something like the opposite of multitasking. Being somewhere else mentally is hiding in some phony, virtual world of planning and calculation. God didn't set us down in the world of elsewhere; He made us to occupy one square foot, give or take, and one thin instant. Here and now. It's so simple, and so difficult to accept in this modern world.

I began to reflect on how seldom I lived in the moment—and the abrupt ways I was made aware of the fact. There was an occasion when I was lecturing Mike, my middle son. He was just a little guy at the time, and he had crossed some minor boundary. I was explaining to him the error of his ways, and of course he did what kids do. He stared at some spot on the floor between his two tennis shoes.

I did what dads do. I repeated the words I'd learned from my own father. "Mike, look me in the eye when I'm speaking to you."

"Why should I?" he asked. I recognized the tone of defiance and figured now I had one more problem to correct: attitude. But before I could open my mouth, he continued, "Because you never look at *me* when I'm talking to *you*—you're always looking at your computer."

Busted. I felt a sudden deflation.

A child will tell you something like that. But how many adults will be that honest? How many other people, including those I cherish most, had I devalued by being too preoccupied, too *elsewhere*, to make eye contact?

I came to realize that phones and gadgets had become obstacles to real eye contact and real conversation and real interaction with real, in-the-moment people. The adventure of life is in those complete, honest, and unreserved interactions, even when they're messy. *Especially* when they're messy.

But those are happening less frequently. Every eight minutes, according to research, we're checking our phones for calls, e-mails, and texts. We respond to the little notification tones the way Pavlov's dog listened to the bell for feeding.

After Rich and I had made the bet about going into airplane mode, I noticed something very strange. Off and on, through the day, I felt the familiar vibration in my pocket, as if my phone were present and doing its thing. In reality, that phone was buried in my backpack and powered off. But the idea of it had become so powerful and the conditioning had become so pervasive that my imagination was creating the sensation of the phone and intruding in my day—much like the man who "feels" his amputated leg itching.

Later, I read about "cell phone separation anxiety." But who would want to seek therapy for that one?

I returned to the States and regarded my phone in a new light.

Now, having experienced the joy of separation, I could be objective about my relationship with the little plastic box.

When you think about it, e-mails and texts rarely inspire any kind of happy response. If I had thirty-eight e-mail messages, I would groan. When was I going to catch up with all those? Yet if the opposite happened, and I had no messages, I would feel some odd sense of rejection. Thus, the two flavors served are "too much" and "too little." There's no such thing as "just right."

And really, how satisfying is a conversation by e-mail or text anyway—even by video using Skype, for that matter? Our communication has increased in quantity, but certainly not quality. In contrast, I've had many conversations with new friends in rural Africa. We share the same little patch of earth and the same moment, and even with language difficulties, we seem to communicate more fully and in more satisfying ways. There's no hurry and no hidden agendas. The present moment is full and it's outstanding! My friends look me in the eye, and they listen very attentively to every word I say, as if it's a privilege. Best of all, I find myself doing the same.

Presence—the lesson I learned in hermitage. There's tremendous power in the simple gift of full and undivided attention.

Now, during airplane mode, I thought to myself, *How wonderful would it be if I could attend fully and thoughtfully to every person I speak to, from now on, wherever I happen to be? No looking past them to see who else is in the room. No glancing at a watch or a phone. Just a commitment to the idea that you and I share this moment, and for the duration of it you have 100 percent of me.*

I've heard it said many times that Americans own the watches while Africans own the time. That now makes perfect sense. I discovered that if I asked an African how he was doing, I should be very serious and honest about my question, because it would be answered in full. To ask, "How are you doing?" in many African cultures is to present a very deep and personal question. Don't expect to hear, "Great! Couldn't be better." The answer will be thorough and honest.

Tekle Selassie, my friend from Ethiopia, had the reverse experience upon moving to the United States to attend college in Minnesota. His dorm held a welcome party for him, and the greeting was warm. But the next morning, when a dorm mate passed by, he said, "Hey, Tekle, how are you?" and kept walking, even as Tekle was a few words into his reply.

What have I done to give offense? he wondered. *Nobody would ask such a question and refuse to hear the reply, unless he intended a grave insult.*

But then, he hadn't learned about our world of distractions and how it keeps all our interactions on the most superficial of levels. In Africa, there's nothing to get in the way. What Swensen calls margin is a reality. Time enslaves nobody and is shared luxuriously.

Again, I thought, *What if I could learn to practice that skill with my wife? We talk over dinner, and she tells me about the little hurts she has experienced during the day. Then she looks into my eyes and sees that I'm far away, probably surfing some inner to-do list. And I've actually piled on one more little hurt. Why can't I gift her with my presence, my devoted attention?*

In time, I would come to see how the frenzy of accomplishment controls our nation's capital. In DC, there is caffeine in the air, an adrenaline rush through the day. In my trips there—which became as many as my trips to Africa, as the two intertwined—I would see an atmosphere of urgency exceeding even my own. I told one friend in Congress, "Everything here is so urgent that nothing is truly important." And I've gotten caught up in it during visits—kind of the anti-Africa.

If I could keep busy, I'd believed—if I could conquer agendas and lists and sets of goals—I could feel good about myself. I had determined my place in the pecking order. The faster I ran, the greater my importance. I know I would have kept stepping on the gas until there was no more gas to give, and I would have fallen over in exhaustion, wondering why I never crossed the finish line, why I never "got there." And why I felt so lonely, having forgotten how to share moments with people I loved. Driven people are souls in exile.

I stopped and smelled no roses. I declined to stop and thank God for the day, because I had yet to fill that day to capacity. Which is what I thought He wanted.

Busyness and doing—the themes of life as I knew it.

Intentionality and being—the themes of the life I yearned for.

I remember a brief conversation in our culture about flexible work weeks; maybe even getting below forty hours. *Newsweek's* cover projected the arrival of the three-day work week. Other cultures, we observed, made far fewer sacrifices at the altar of career. But in our brave new world, computers would free us up! They would do our heavy thinking and multitasking while we spent extra time with the family. Wasn't that a beautiful dream?

The computers had other ideas. Forty hours? We soon learned we had to be plugged in 24/7 if we didn't want some other eager beaver taking our jobs. Everyone needed to be "on call" round the clock. So-called social media upped the ante. The idea was to flood the world with promotion of yourself and your product through constant tweets and status updates, make thousands upon thousands of "friends," even though you'd probably never meet most of them. The day was coming, perhaps, when the word *friend* would give way to *contact*.

On a happy day in my life, I repented. I wanted the kind of friendship I had seen modeled across the sea. I wanted to think through my work rather than rush through it. I wanted to deal with people, not use them. I wanted to touch souls rather than process status updates.

And I realized I desperately needed time to reflect. I didn't want my legacy to be several thousand miles wide and one inch deep.

But I had to wonder how many other people were sharing my

feelings about these things. After all, progress was marching on. No one was saying, "Okay, we've developed enough technology. We've maxed out our busyness. Let's shut down research and development for a couple of decades." The human spirit never ceases to be competitive; it looks for ways to go even faster and do even more.

The time finally came when I retired, at least by definition. I sold my businesses and figured, as most do, that now I would be completely free to reflect, to travel, to think and discuss deeply, and to escape the tyranny of the urgent.

So, why did I find myself busier than ever? I still needed more margin, more time intentionally filled with nothing. I began to develop obligation-free zones—periods of time in which I would not be tied down by anything or anyone—as a discipline in life. If God wanted me, He knew where to find me. I had never struggled to offer Him the treasure of my finances. But that was fool's gold, in a way. Now I was going to find out if I could tithe the true treasure: my time.

At this point in my life, wisdom has become a goal. I understand that it will come only through the deeper reflection and soul-searching that came when I made myself utterly available to God, just as I was going to be utterly available to my wife and my closest friends. Wisdom can only grow through presence.

I couldn't help but notice that of all the Ten Commandments, the only one that contains the word *holy* is the fourth, which says, "Remember the Sabbath day by keeping it holy" (Exodus 20:8). It is not a suggestion but a commandment that we *do no work* on that seventh day, in the imitation of God Himself. Here is an order from on high that we should find utterly delightful—the command to shut down and rest for a while. And yet I believe it's the most widely ignored commandment of them all. We are one strange creation.

Reflecting on the airplane mode challenge with Rich, I realized it was about more than a friendly bet. I wanted my wife to recognize the difference. I wanted her to realize I was feeling a little of the same liberation I felt on my trip. Why should I have to go halfway around the world to change what lies between my ears? I knew I'd always need Africa. But I also knew it would be thrilling to take a little of Africa home with me.

Slowing down, I resolved to better experience the gracious rhythm and flow of living fully in the present.

When it comes to all the noise of my life, I realized, I'm not the victim but the perpetrator. I do it to myself. I'm so often chasing the wrong rabbit, as so well illustrated by Simon Guillebaud in *Choose Life*. He observes the mechanics of greyhound racing, where a man in a box controls an electronic rabbit, keeping it just in front of the dogs—close enough to make them run full-out. But on one occasion, something shorted out, and the rabbit exploded. The dogs, confronted by a smoking mess of wires and panels, were confused. Two of them slammed into a wall, breaking ribs. One began chasing its tail. Others howled, while some settled down in the dust. None finished the race.

Chasing rabbits is an image of our world, where people madly pursue that which they don't realize is fake. Sometimes we need the whole thing to go up in smoke before we realize our wasted motion. Maybe we can learn to run a different race entirely.

My own pursuit of abandoning the urgent has mixed results. Like breaking any addiction, it's heavy lifting. But I'm slowly yet surely adjusting to the tremendous blessing of being more unplugged from the ever increasing and often incoherent noise of the society we live in. More and more, I'm realizing the wisdom of one of the shortest but most poignant verses in Scripture: "Be still, and know that I am God" (Psalm 46:10).

8

Losing Self

Wherever I Go ... There I Am

◆━◆━◆

Masquerade

Through sacred gates of silence I pass into a different world.
of silence, of solitude ... of safety.
A place of peace yet painful revelation.
No longer on stage ... displaying all my gifts with a bow,
I am forced to humbly address the Giver.
And the imposter retreats ... Not gone, but in temporary hiding.
In this Cathedral of quietness I, too, am hiding.
In the solitude and stillness I see clearly the madness of my life.
I see the imposter who needs attention and applause
and the ambition behind the lure and lie of accomplishment.
Bone tired from the stress of so many of the imposters pretenses
...
Chasing the mindless urgent which often triumphs the essential.
A relentless quest of muchness as I hurry past the sacred.
My will be done ...
Rediscovering the broken places in my life;
large wounds with superficial Band-Aids.
And my clever masks are tenderly removed.
The promise of a distant sunset filters through
the sentry of ancient Oaks.
A reminder of the Covenant.

The Giver smiles and with Him comes the truth
that sets me free.
I am safe.
Now it's the imposter who is imprisoned ...
Banished to his rightful place of shame. Not me.
My confidence is restored.
Not in myself but the Healer.
My thanks is reflected by a new song placed in my heart
that only the angels can hear.[1]

Have you ever realized you were sick of somebody? That you and that person needed a little space apart?

I felt that way about myself. And I wondered how many other people must feel exactly the same—about *me*. But what can I do? Where can I go to get away? Because wherever I go—there I am. They say the grass is greener on the other side, but my experience is that it's not. Because once I get there ... there I am.

In terms of getting fed up with myself, I could only ask myself, *What took you so long? It's not as if your worst traits were anything new.* And I replied to myself that Myself had a point. (He can be very abrasive.)

Jesus knew I'd have this issue, and if I didn't have it, I'd *really* have a problem. As Pogo, the old comic strip opossum, once said, "We have met the enemy and he is us." But Jesus said it better. He made plenty of statements about the need to lose oneself and to put oneself last. All those teachings sound wonderful if you ignore the fact that they're nearly impossible to live by. Even those not too enamored with the Bible claim the Golden Rule as wisdom, but they haven't found it very practical either.

If you've been paying attention up to now, you know that self is a big issue for me, and I came to the place where I needed to get it out of the way, at least enough to figure out what really counted for the second half of my life. Like many others, I'd determined that the first part of life is a quest for "success," of a sort. The second part of life, I agreed, was about "significance." But here again, how do we decide what that means? We can all agree that money and power and all those things aren't what they're cracked up to be. So, what does it mean to be significant?

I decided it meant making a positive difference in the lives of others, reflecting more, and a few other things. But here, I found, was the problem. *Significance* gets all tangled up with that issue of *self*. What I mean by that is that it becomes very easy to make too big a deal out of my importance in the world. Significance can become just another form of pride.

I found that often, my quest to be relevant, to be earnestly helpful, was just ambition in a trickier disguise. The big reveal for me had been that I was finding my identity and sense of purpose in keeping busy. I was that guy on the old variety show (Ed Sullivan, if you're old enough to remember) juggling plates. "Look how many plates I can juggle! Look how fine and expensive some of the plates are!"

Maybe focusing on Africa, for example, was just the same juggling act with more exotic plates. In a way, you could have viewed it as a more devious cry for attention and affirmation, because most of the people in my crowd were juggling more expensive plates. Maybe I was just shifting my focus to hear the world's applause or to feel better about myself.

Note the last word of that paragraph. I realized that no matter what I do, no matter where I go—to Africa or to Washington, DC, or anywhere in between—there I am. I am me. And by my personal scoreboard, that's the biggest problem I'll ever face.

I struggled with this point, because I knew my heart was filled with the right motives. I also knew that if I did a good deed, the bottom line was that someone benefited from it. If I could do anything at all to help establish a self-sustaining medical station in eastern Congo, did it really matter? Wouldn't it be the very essence of self-absorption to withdraw from a good act because I had detected mixed motives?

Sure. These things needed to be done, and they would be done, but the motive part mattered too. It mattered to me. I needed to understand that I could fight the good fight for God's kingdom right up to the gates of hell, but at any given time, the most potentially dangerous enemy could be viewed in the mirror.

Most of all, I needed to see that God always got the credit—that I continued to be a billboard for Him and not for me.

Kris and I had a conversation about this. I set personal goals each year, and the top one never changes: do a better job of following Jesus and being obedient to His teachings. And one year, I really felt like I was making some inroads toward these goals. Kris smiled warmly and told me I had become "partners with Jesus." I really liked that—kind of a "God is my copilot" thing. Then Kris added, "The only problem is that you are the *managing* partner."

Ouch.

Copilot sounds great, but we needed to switch seats.

I thought about the enduring battle of self and tried to internalize some of what the Bible says about who we are. After all, if we could see ourselves as God sees us—no larger but no smaller, either—we'd have just the right self-concept. Here's an example: "What is your life? You are a mist that appears for a little while and then vanishes" (James 4:14). A wisp in the wind. Also, "all people are like grass, and all their glory is like the flowers of the field" (1 Peter 1:24). I knew that what seems powerfully significant to me was just another flower that gave beauty for a few days, only to fade and vanish.

For someone like me, that was a hard truth, because ego was an issue. Someone told me that EGO stands for "edging God out." Monty Sholund used to say that *sin* is defined by its middle letter. But I didn't need to learn any of this from the writings of others. I knew the truth from my own heart.

What I saw, as I looked in that mirror, was someone who magnified his own importance in life whether that came through business or through mission. I couldn't win the war simply through shifting the battlefield. The enemy remained the same, wherever I chose to oppose him.

Confronting this truth gave me a new lens through which to examine who I was and what I was doing. A few years ago, I was asked to be part of the National Prayer Breakfast in the nation's capital. I would be the master of ceremonies for the gathering of the African guests and also chair a number of related events. Of course, the rest of my life was as frantic as usual. This is the problem with lacking margin—when you overbook your life, there is no room for the serendipitous things that God brings your way. You get the schedule and agenda you've predetermined, when God nearly always has one much better.

I simply juggled a little faster, taking on the extra plates and refusing to let go of any of the old ones. And a few days before I was due to fly to Washington, I came down with the flu (sometimes, that's life's way of telling you it's time to slow down a little). Well, I would drink my fluids, "hurry up and rest," and catch that big Prayer Breakfast plate before it hit the floor.

Except I felt worse and worse; I couldn't crawl out of the bed. Not only did it seem evident I couldn't make it to Washington, but it also felt as if this wouldn't be a bad time to update my will. "Lord," I prayed. "You know I need some quick healing! There's no way the show will go on without me." Maybe I would have a miraculous recovery, the very morning of my flight, and it would be another great story for my book someday—a story of what God can do when things look the bleakest.

Because the National Prayer Breakfast *had* to have me, right? I was a nonnegotiable. I laid in bed like Job, suffering my illness and lamenting about the sad fate of those festivities. But Kris handled things with much more grace than Job's wife, who urged him to "curse God and die" (Job 2:9). Kris simply said, "Tell me where to find your agenda for the event."

I told her, and she calmly rang up one of my best buddies, Mike Sime. She knew he was planning to be there too. "Ward is really sick—as sick as I've seen him," she said. "Is there any way you can pinch-hit for him?"

"Absolutely," Mike said. "No problem."

I turned my face to the wall and groaned. Mike was a great guy, but he wasn't *me*. They asked *me*. Didn't everybody understand that?

When I heard how well Mike had done—well, actually, he had done fabulously—I was delighted. I guess. By many accounts, he may have actually been an upgrade.

Serendipity, or what others have expressed as "God moving in mysterious ways," gave Mike a special opportunity to shine and me a special opportunity to learn a valuable lesson from Mike's reflected glory. No one is expendable—certainly not me. I have many plans for Africa and other passions of my life, but if I leave the face of this earth, God has several billion other occupants of the planet to press into service. My ego doesn't have that phrase framed on his desk, but he ought to. Harry Truman's desk plaque said, *The buck stops here.* I need one that says, *Do your thing. Or we'll find somebody else.*

It's a liberating thing to stop carrying the whole world on your shoulders. Finding this out was one more ultimate gift of Africa. I discovered how small, how Western, and how momentary my complex world was. Over there, none of the materialism mattered. My ego and self-importance meant nothing at all to the kind, calm souls that I met. I was just a guy. We spend a lot of our time trying to rise above "just a guy," but there's wisdom in discovering that if we can be that, then God has us right where He wants us. I knew it was time to take off my cape, stop moving faster than a speeding bullet, and begin moving slowly enough to really listen and serve. A friend once told me I speak eighty miles per hour with gusts up to one hundred. I realize I have one mouth and two ears, and a good rule of thumb for me is to use them in appropriate proportion.

Sometimes life has helped me with that goal. Talking about Africa is a great example. Most people who travel there come back with worlds of details they want to share. They find out very quickly that people will smile and be encouraging, but a quick summary will suffice. They don't want to see the whole slide show. I've learned that, to some extent, God didn't give me Africa so I could talk endlessly about it. There's a certain discipline to keeping some things between you and God and knowing that what you've experienced doesn't translate well to cocktail parties and church chatter.

But every now and then, I find a willing victim, somebody who actually wants to hear more. I don't need much encouragement to fill their request. It happened at a dinner for African guests and others interested in Africa. I found myself sitting beside a quiet American man who introduced himself as Richard and began asking me questions. I talked a little about my trips to Africa, and he showed real interest. "Tell me more about that," he said, smiling.

"Do you really mean that? Because I can definitely do it."

"Sure. I'd love to hear about what you've experienced." And he asked some specific questions that proved his curiosity was truly piqued. The more I told him, the more questions came. He'd interject comments such as, "That's fascinating," and, "I had no idea!" And I was getting to share my whole dog and pony show. I'd found the perfect companion for the dinner.

The only problem was that the evening ended too quickly. I was just getting warmed up! I shook my new friend's hand and said, "I've really enjoyed getting to know you, Richard. But now we have to leave, so I'll tell you what. I've written two books on Africa. If you'll just give me your address, I'd be pleased to see you a copy of each."

He said, "I'd love that." He reached into his pocket, then handed me a business card. The name on it was Richard Foster.

"Excuse me," I said. "You can't be *the* Richard Foster—the author?"

He was, of course. Foster was and is one of my heroes of faith. His best-known book is *Celebration of Discipline*, which concerns some of the very issues I was grappling with at the time—prayer, reflection, personal growth. *Christianity Today* named it one of the top ten books of the twentieth century. He wrote one of my favorite books on prayer, and he'd had a huge influence on my spiritual formation. And I'd been talking his ear off, as if I were educating a pupil. Not that he'd been offended, of course, because he'd simply been using both ears and deferring the deployment of his mouth. He was proving the sincerity of his written words.

It's possible I told him some things he didn't know about my subject, but I know there was also plenty of material he already knew. But never once did he say, "Yeah, yeah, so I've heard." He listened attentively and asked questions that proved his attention. He was fully present in the moment.

I was too, of course, but only one of us walked away with new light. My mind reeled with questions I'd have loved to have asked him. And perhaps there would be other occasions for that, now that the ice was broken. But I'd just blown a brilliant opportunity, an up-close-and-personal encounter with one of my genuine heroes.

Self is the issue on occasions like that one. Unselfish people listen naturally, reflexively. They have wisdom, and that's no coincidence. They've come across it by knowing how to get that ego out of the way so they can listen and learn and live.

Richard Foster was, for me, a grand eminence. But on how many occasions have I been in the presence of God Himself and showed no desire to hear rather than speak? What is really more important—talking to God or listening to Him? What we can tell Him is basically nothing at all. What He can tell us is infinite.

I have another one of those witty friends who said, "The most fascinating thing about all your stories is that you're in every one of them."

Ouch.

Maybe I have an excuse for not wanting to listen, if you consider what people are saying to me.

As I studied more of the words of Jesus, I didn't see much of this "strong sense of self." Yes, we are to love our neighbors as we love ourselves, and that implies a basic self-love. But as I came to understand His teachings, the problem is that that sense of self we present to the world is based upon the values of the world: people, performance, possessions, and power. I wondered if I needed to take a ride in an empty cab from time to time. Jesus, we are told, "emptied Himself, taking the form of a bond-servant" (Philippians 2:7 NASB). He came in the form of a helpless baby, born to obscure parents in a nowhere town. He left on a cross. If anyone had every right to be "full of himself," so to speak, it was the Son of God. But He modeled selflessness.

I needed to learn what it meant to empty myself, or at the very least to get over myself. But where to begin?

I found that I grew most tired of being who I was at the very times when my self-importance was at its highest levels. There were times when I found it hard to seek God because I was consumed by my own plans and ideas. As always, He had places to go with me and things to do, but I was way out in front, running ahead of Him. I was setting His agenda.

Just learning to be quiet was the first step. Trips to the hermitage helped with that, and when that wasn't possible, I could simply learn to default to God in my thoughts, putting space between my conception of His greatness and my own little words and deeds. It was a tough discipline, something that never seemed to become easier. But in time I found that, on my better days, I could feel the Spirit of God filling the void between His majesty and my humbled self. Then I could live in the hope that maybe, just maybe, I was transformed a tiny bit closer toward His likeness. In other words, I could experience just a glimmer of His resurrection power.

I tried to read all that I could on surrendering self. There's not a great deal of literature on that subject, because, frankly, it's not very popular. I know a lot more people who are less interested in surrendering than in declaring victory for themselves. Richard Foster's writings, of course, were a terrific help, particularly because I had experienced the sincerity of them firsthand. In that one conversation, he modeled self-emptying, attentive listening, and simple kindness. How encouraging to know it *could* be done.

I came across the words of theologian Richard Rohr, the Franciscan priest who wrote *Falling Upward: A Spirituality for the Two Halves of Life*. He also wrote the following meditation:

> Spiritual surrender is not giving up, which is the way we usually understand the term. Surrender is entering the present moment, and what is right in front of you, fully and without resistance or attempts at control. In that sense, surrender is almost the exact opposite of giving up. In fact, it is a being given to![2]

These words gave me hope, because they linked my idea of presence with the ideas of humility and surrender. Africa had all but forced me into the present moment in the way described here. Rohr calls it "aweism." When we comprehend that everything before us is a miracle, we can find recovery from any disease of the mind.

Experienced pilgrims of the deeper life won't be surprised to find that I also discovered Oswald Chambers and his classic book, *My Utmost for His Highest*. It's an old book that only seems to touch greater numbers of hearts as time goes on. The wearier people become, the more disappointed with their own lives they find themselves, the more solace they find in this little devotional.

One of Chambers' statements hit me right between the eyes: the point that we "fail because we place our own holiness above our desire to know God."[3] Again, he showed me that even when we're certain we're taking the right steps, even in prayer itself, we can still be ruled and ruined by self. What I needed was to seek God, period. I needed to forget myself, if only for a few moments, and immerse myself in the worship of Him—a very hard thing to do for a crusty old driven achiever like me. Chambers wrote, "God cannot deliver me while my interest is merely in my own character."[4]

Above all, I began to focus on what Jesus said about the path of following Him: "Whoever wants to be my disciple must deny themselves and take up their cross daily and follow me. For whoever wants to save their life will lose it, but whoever loses their life for me will save it" (Luke 9:23–24). Matthew and Mark offer these same words, but it is Luke who adds the word *daily*.

I considered the difference that one little word makes. If I had only the other two Gospels, I could convince myself that this idea of discipleship was a *transaction*. As a businessman, I know about transactions. I give you something, you give me something. I'd like to think I could trade something to Jesus and be a disciple. But the word *daily* tells me it's more of a process. Not only that, but experience has taught me the same thing. It's not a one-time price to be paid any more than going to the gym is a one-time event. You have to keep going back to transact a workout or the whole effect is loss. I have to keep taking up my cross or I lose all that I'm trying to experience of Jesus.

For me, losing myself means first acknowledging and then intentionally shedding the various masks and disguises I so naturally wear. The default is often to become a chameleon assuming different attitudes and associated behaviors, depending upon the people I'm with. I take on different personalities in order to fit in. That's something like the antithesis of "to thine own self be true."

Brennan Manning, in his remarkable book *Abba's Child*, has

an amazing and equally disturbing chapter called "The Imposter." It speaks at length about the false self who is typically created by us early in life to protect us from hurts of all sorts. "This false self serves us well then, but after that use is completed can often continue to whisper things in our ear that are no longer true or helpful. What was once a blessing is now a curse."

Maybe it's not just about "losing myself" but also getting rid of all the counterfeit selves and hanging on for dear life to the only real one.

That's hard. But on the positive end, it's calming to me to know that I can always go back, no matter how I fail later in the day, no matter the fact that I let my ego trip me up again, no matter the fact that I feel like the aspiring disciple Jesus might have said no thanks to. His mercies, we read, are new every morning. So, no matter what has come before, I can come before Him, enter a spirit of reverence and learn a bit more about self-denial and the emptying of me.

There's also my hermitage. I thank God for bringing Pacem in Terris into my life. There, I know I can be alone and silent. I can look through the great plate glass window and be worshipful before God's creation. And the more of Him I take in, the more of me that empties out. I rest. I reflect. All my facades and defense mechanisms peel away like the layers of one very stubborn onion. Deep inside, I discover that wisp of a soul, that scared but eager creation that is the real me, whom only God knows.

If I can accomplish that, I can elude the smothering clutches of self in favor of the loving embrace of the divine. It feels good, though I know tomorrow is another day. Just as God's tender mercies are renewed, so must be my acceptance of them.

It's not easy for me to find the right balance of the ever present tension between trusting God and using my talents. By grace I get a fresh start each morning—to pick up my cross and follow.

9

What Is Truth?

And Does God Speak ... Really?

> "What is truth?"
> —PILATE, JOHN 18:38

> Our failure to hear His voice when we want to is due to
> the fact that we do not in general want to hear it,
> that we want it only when we think we need it.
> —DALLAS WILLARD

There are friends, close friends, and business partners. When someone fills those last two categories, you have to be pretty comfortable with them. You love them, you respect them, and sometimes you're close enough to have epic, heated arguments.

This was Jeff Bird, my business partner, and this was one of those occasions. We were really going at it over a particularly thorny theological issue. After I gave what I thought was the definitive answer on the issue, he turned and said, "Ward, it doesn't matter what you think!"

Talk about an arrogant statement. Just as I was about to fire back, he said, "From you or anybody. Just because somebody thinks something is true, that doesn't make it true."

I stopped and listened more closely. "For any issue, any question, there's one truth," he continued. "No more, no less. One. And you or I might be absolutely sure we have a good handle on what that truth is. We can be utterly sincere about it, but sincerely wrong."

Jeff was 100 percent correct.

Rick Warren has said that truth isn't determined by a popularity contest. A lie is a lie regardless of who believes it. It's the same with an unpopular truth. We don't get to vote on whether to accept the law of gravity; it's not subject to any ballots. I don't believe in aging, but it believes in me. And if gravity and aging aren't just guidelines but laws, can't the same be true of more abstract principles, such as issues of right and wrong?

Rick Warren is also fond of saying that we care too much about being on the right side of culture when the only thing that counts is whether we're on the right side of God.

I've often thought of that incredible moment in John 18 when Jesus stood before Pontius Pilate. It was the night when the powers that be were passing sentence on Him. Jesus told Pilate that His reason for coming into this world was to testify to the truth. As an elite, classically educated Roman of the ruling class, he regarded the peasant rabbi before him and asked in John 18:38, "What is truth?"

But I noticed that Pilate didn't wait for an answer. There's still a lot of that going around—throwing up our hands and saying, "Sure, whatever. Who knows what the truth is? Your truth and my truth might be different."

But Jesus said He *was* the truth. Meaning everybody's truth. I've tried to take that seriously, and make Him my true north in my search for truth. Not "my truth," "your truth," or "what works for me," but *the* truth in any question.

I believe Jesus alone knows the heart and will of God, and as He told Pilate, He came so that we could have some idea of it too.

Then there's 1 Corinthians 1:20: "Has not God made foolish the wisdom of the world?" There's an idea in the Bible that God's wisdom and the world's version of wisdom aren't compatible. This is why the world sees Christianity as foolishness, as Paul pointed out. It's also why I look at the world sometimes and its ideas seem crazy to me.

You can become the world's best-educated man, possess all the knowledge one human memory can contain, and you'd have no advantage in finding godly wisdom. God's truth must be procured in God's way. In my life, I'd gone to church for years. I'd sought God, and yes, I'd learned a certain amount of biblical truth. But not until my life changed did I allow that wisdom to flow into my life. I had knowledge but not the wisdom of the Word.

I began to get glimpses of truth, and I noticed more often that people would talk about "hearing God's voice." I had questions about that. I've found that bumpy, dusty roads in the third world are wonderful places for asking these questions. There is room for the mind to stretch out, and there are far fewer distractions.

I was on one such road with my friends Rich Voelbel, George "Pokot" Fulton, and our Ethiopian buddy, Tekle Selassie. We were discussing spiritual things, and I asked, "How do we actually have a conversation with God?"

I explained that I'd often heard people say things such as "God spoke to me" or "God placed a burden on my heart" or "I've had a word from God on this subject." I never wanted to break into such a moment and say, "What does He sound like? Did you actually hear a voice? What kind of accent does God have?" It would seem irreverent and, I admit, it might also be a little embarrassing to admit that I wasn't hearing God's voice too. I'm sure a lot of people have done what I always did, and kept their mouths shut—continuing to wonder just how one hears the voice of God.

But now we were in Africa. The dusty roads had broken down barriers and allowed us to be real, and I felt a freedom to ask my questions.

There were a few moments of silence, then Tekle began to speak with a kind of quiet authority. "I believe you can listen to God in three different ways," he said. "The first is through other people. Many times God will place people along the pathways of our lives for distinct purposes. They are there to speak into our lives with truth we need to hear. They could be friends or total strangers, but we learn to listen at all times for a message that seems to resonate for us. And we may or may not realize that God has spoken, because it came through a human voice."

I hadn't thought of that. I'd assumed that God speaking to me had to be a one-on-one arrangement, and if I didn't physically "hear" something, there would at least be an "impression" somewhere between my ears. Tekle's observation opened for me a whole new world of hearing from God.

"The second way," he said, "is an obvious one. We talk to God through prayer, but the important issue here is that *we also must listen*. As we learned from our friends in Ethiopia, the problem with most Americans is that they like to do all the talking, even when they pray. I think many people don't know how to set aside time just to be still—particularly in such a busy and frantic culture as that of the United States."

This I understood. I've often struggled to be still and to listen.

"And the third way is?" I said.

"Through Scripture," he replied. "A wonderful way to hear God. You can speak to Him and hear from Him very intimately, simply by reading from His Word."

This, too, was something to think about. I had often approached the Bible as a mere book—or, actually, as a *series* of sixty-six books—and felt guilty when I found myself responding in boredom. The history was confusing, the culture seemed remote and irrelevant, and there were times when I frankly couldn't see why so many people seemed enamored with this ancient volume. I needed maps, a dictionary, a 1611 King James decoder ring— reading the Bible was a chore.

Yet when I begin to approach the Bible as one deep, unified dialogue with God and acknowledge the real possibility of it interacting with whatever was happening in my life, Scripture comes to life. Instead of thinking, *Here's that old book of history and laws and doctrines*, I began to think, *Here is a place where God is waiting to meet me and talk to me.* It's almost like a coffee shop where I might catch breakfast with a good friend.

But this "coffee shop" is filled with a rich pageant of things and places and people that are, all at the same time, about "then" and about *right now*, about "them" and about *me*. If the experiences happened to King David or the apostle Paul, that's one thing (and usually *interesting*, once I give it a chance); but when I can look into David or Paul's lives and see my own world and my own issues, Scripture becomes an anointed source of wisdom. The Psalms and Proverbs are as relevant today as they were thousands of years ago and speak directly into specific things happening around me.

And, read this way, Scripture does come alive—so much so that the personal messages shifted and changed with my life. By now, I've read through the Bible—Old and New Testaments— many times, yet it's rather shocking to keep coming to verses that didn't seem to be there last time! Or, at least now those same verses and passages step forward to speak about this particular week in my life. I think, *How did I miss that before?* And I know that the point is, the Bible misses *nothing* in my life. I don't read it as much as it reads me. That's a very different experience.

Monty Sholund helped me begin to learn how to hear God through the Scriptures. He said, "When you're listening to God through the Scriptures, be on the lookout for four different things. With each chapter you read, you should be able to find a teaching, a promise, a key verse, and a warning."

I'll have to admit I was skeptical, based on my experiences with Scripture. The Bible seemed to be all over the place stylistically. I was fascinated to learn that the New Testament books following the four Gospels are ordered only by their length, from the longest to shortest until the final book, Revelation. Psalms had one format, books of history had another, and there was absolutely no similarity between, say, a letter from Paul and a Gospel account. How could all these styles contain each of those four things?

Yet to my amazement, Monty was right. Since he told me that, I've been able to find at least one of each—teaching, promise, key verse, and warning—in most readings. And again, this was a game changer in my Bible-reading sessions. You've figured out by now that I'm a list guy, and I like having a set strategy to help me study a passage. Monty's system gave me an approach, a to-do list if you will, for any chapter of Scripture. I could read *actively* that way, and the truth began to unfold itself before me as I brought that effort to my study times.

Sometimes I pull my nose out of the Bible and turn on the radio or television, or check the Internet. The contrast makes its own statement. The noise and chaos of the world come to us through never-ending units of "breaking news," nearly all of it alarming or disturbing in some way. Sensationalism is now the guiding principle of the news fed to the people, and it's no wonder depression and mood issues have reached epic scales.

Yet the Scriptures quietly continue speaking the truth, often free of sensation. Scripture tells me love is the best thing in the universe, that God is in control, that grace trumps bitterness, that integrity still makes for a good life. These are wildly useful truths flying under the world's radar, truths that harness all the world's chaos into something that makes sense—a place where God can be known and where evil never writes the final chapter.

Beneath the storm, or perhaps in the eye of that storm, God quietly continues to speak truth through the people I know, the prayers I utter, and the pages I read of His Word. It confounds the wise. It's why Jesus exclaimed, "Do you have eyes but fail to see, and ears but fail to hear?" (Mark 8:18). The truth isn't going anywhere; God is not silent. I simply need to tune in my spiritual senses, my "receptors." To do that, I know I have to give up my pride and self-importance. Jesus told us to come to Him in the way of little children, and that frankly wasn't going to be something at the top of my agenda. A little child knows how to keep it simple. Kids know how to trust, how to believe. That doesn't come easily for me.

Once, when His disciples had enjoyed a wonderful break-through, Jesus stood before them and prayed, "I praise you, Father, Lord of heaven and earth, because you have hidden these things from the wise and learned, and revealed them to little children. … Many prophets and kings wanted to see what you see but did not see it, and to hear what you hear but did not hear it" (Luke 10:21, 24).

Again, two tracks of "wisdom," one from heaven and one from the world. The "prophets and kings" of our time wrestle over what they call the truth. Different brands of churches fight over the niceties of their versions of "right doctrine." Every issue is up for debate and has its adherents ready for all-out war over their inter-pretation. Why don't they just turn to Scripture? Is it that simple?

I wish it were. I've found that in any of the volatile issues of our day, I can open Scripture and find a passage to support one side, then a different passage to support the other. I just have to be selective enough. Why isn't Scripture helping me as I do that? Where is the voice of God at that time? The problem is that if I'm out to bolster a position, I'm not seeking truth, but seeking "proof texts." I'm on the front lines, glaring at my enemy while reaching behind me to God and saying, "Hand me some ammunition."

Maybe I need more often to start with the truth, through all the ways God gives it to me, and then just go where it leads me. In a world quickly becoming more and more alienated, I realize I need truth without agenda or manipulation and only God and His Word are capable of providing that.

10

Coin of Another Realm

Defining True Riches

Q: How much money did John D. Rockefeller
leave behind when he died?

A: All of it.

—ANONYMOUS

It is not the man who has too little,
but the man who craves more that is poor.

—SENECA

Monty Sholund helped me learn to listen to God through Scripture. But there was one day when it was a little difficult to listen to Monty. His subject was *me*, and I had strong opinions on that topic.

For some reason, he was giving an elaborate review of my business career—two thumbs up, rave reviews. Why wouldn't I want to hear this? For one thing, I knew the man was up to something. There was no way he'd spend all this time praising my work unless there was a catch somewhere.

He hit all the highlights, beginning with my earliest successes in the insurance business, then moving to the period when I founded an employee benefits insurance company, then a "boutique" insurance and agent planning firm. There was high praise for my every move, and I'd stopped eating and started watching him closely, waiting for the other shoe to drop.

"You always made the right moves," he said. "Every step of the way, your decisions were brilliant."

Pause.

"What I can't figure out is how you pulled off the most brilliant move of them all—the one that made all your maneuvers possible."

He stopped to take a leisurely bite.

I watched with one eyebrow uplifted.

He paused for a moment, which always meant trouble, then said, "So, tell me, Ward: How in the world were you able to orchestrate being born into the affluent suburb of Edina, Minnesota, to two terrific parents?"

I stared at him for a moment, then we were both laughing. Point taken. I had no answer for his question, of course.

If life is a baseball game, we're all born somewhere along the base path. Some are born halfway between third and home. I wasn't quite that fortunate, but the point holds. We like to tell stories of lifting ourselves up by our own bootstraps, completely taking for granted the starting point—which we had nothing to do with. You could be born into a third-world village ravaged by famine and disease, or you could be born with a silver spoon in your mouth with every advantage awaiting you, including education, medical care, and maybe dibs on a great career opening. You're born where you're born.

Who but God knows what purposes guide these things? The door by which we enter Earth is the ultimate roll of the dice, at least from our limited perspective. I've held extremely impoverished children in villages like the little girl I described in chapter 2. Looking into those eyes, I wondered what placed me in my position and this suffering child in hers. Before my paradigm shift in Africa, I would never have given a thought to all this. I simply accepted my immense head start on the base paths and bore down for home.

As my African experiences stuck with me, I began to regard my possessions and attainments in a different way. The word *my* became less important to me. It had all come into my hands too easily, hadn't it? The "brilliant decisions" Monty had described (with tongue just barely in cheek) were possible because of my opportunities. Many other men and women would have done similar things or more in my place.

That idea had radical implications for the idea of who I was, and what God had to do with it. Nothing is ultimately mine.

What we call possessions are, in fact, gifts. Our society celebrates personal achievement, entrepreneurship, and the athletics of climbing the ladder of success. No perspective is generally offered outside our own efforts. But it's all Monopoly money—it's dealt us, we do our best with it, and then after the game, it all goes back in the box.

After I began to think about these things, I noticed how often the subject arises in Scripture. The word given for our role is *stewards*. The meaning is something like the teenager's job, when he house-sits in the mansion while the wealthy owner is abroad. He lives the good life for a few days and can pretend he's a big shot. He swims in the pool and watches the TV with the huge screen and great sound system. But he's not the owner, and the real point is how well he takes care of the property.

Leo Tolstoy, who became a Christian late in life after a "God moment" of his own, wrote a story called "How Much Land Does a Man Require?" In it, a man is told he can have all the land he encircles by foot in one day. He begins his walk and, as you'd expect, his circle becomes wider and wider due to his greed for the properties he passes.

As the sun begins to go down, he discovers he is far afield from the starting point to which he must circle back. He sprints the rest of the way and makes it, to the applause of many—only to drop dead from overexertion. It turns out he needed only the six feet of earth that was required to bury him.

He's much like the man in Jesus' parable who believes he owns his prosperous farm and can lie back and enjoy himself. "'You fool,' God tells him. "'This very night your life will be demanded from you. Then who will get what you have prepared for yourself?'" (Luke 12:20).

I came to understand that ownership is not only an illusion in the spiritual sense, therefore, but an unhealthy one I didn't want for myself. I also had to consider the idea of stewardship—that my things were to be well maintained for the *true* owner. And to that end, I knew that Jesus said, in the same passage, that to whom much has been given, much will be expected (Luke 12:48). Accountability is paramount.

That was one habit of Jesus' that gave me a good bit of discomfort. He seemed always to be implying some kind of reckoning—the moment when the wealthy owner comes back to inspect the mansion and see how the teenager cared for it. Since it doesn't seem to happen in this life, I had to figure it happens somewhere on the other side—a judgment day that was a kind of "performance review" for earthly investors. Yet in a seeming paradox, we are told time and time again by Jesus that we can only be saved by grace.

I also found that these scriptural ideas were reassuring, not threatening, in the long run. They removed a certain burden from my shoulders. Money, the greatest false god of our culture, has a tremendous hold on us. It causes untold anxiety, while giving us much less joy than we ever expect of it.

I think about my possessions, including our lovely home of thirty years in the woods outside Minneapolis—or even our little family cabin on Whitefish Lake in northern Minnesota. Now, with greater perspective, I could see and accept that the time would come, within a generation or two, that these properties and buildings would pass into the hands of others. I'm a citizen of another world, only passing through. The earth and the sky and the seas remain (but even these, just for a time). Mortality loosens our grip, no matter how tight, and strips away all our holdings. Again, an elaborate board game. All the tokens, all the little houses and hotels, and all the colorful money go back in the box for future players.

When I first grasped this, I felt small and insignificant. Then I realized that I had things precisely backward. In actuality, I'm far too significant to be defined by these tawdry possessions. I am a child of God, heir to His kingdom, destined for eternal life. And realizing that, I can clutch a little less desperately. Maybe I don't need to sweat so much today, grasping that last dollar. I have other fish to fry. When I think about it that way, I feel liberated.

Perhaps you've heard, as I have, that Jesus had more to say about money and possessions than any other topic—fairly amazing for a teacher of "spiritual" things. If He found the topic so urgent, then perhaps I should too. I need to approach it the way He did. To that end, I have to think about what Jesus considered as true wealth.

A key mention of it comes in that perplexing story of the rich young ruler. This wealthy man comes to Jesus claiming to have kept all the commandments. (Who can say whether that's true? I've never met someone who did.) He wants to know what else he should do to "inherit eternal life." Jesus gives him a nice three-step formula. First, sell all you own; second, give the proceeds to the poor; third, come and follow Him.

This is such a provocative recommendation that it's easy for us to gloss over the result Jesus predicts: "You will have treasure in heaven." There it is: heavenly treasure.

By saying this to a man whom the world would consider rich, the implication is clear: the man has no spiritual wealth. *If* he will do what Jesus says, *then* he will have it.

I read that one, pondered it, and understood the greater point the way most people do. It wasn't a condemnation of money, but an indication that earthly wealth does have the power to blind us to other kinds of blessings. The man showed that by turning and walking away. Wealth was not the problem; the addiction to it was.

These insights were fine, but all it really clarified was the truth of earthly treasure. I still wanted to know what exactly "treasure in heaven" might be. Though certain, it's not a passport to heaven. A close friend of mine, who is also a Catholic priest, was raising money for an inner-city school. He related this story: While he was at lunch one day, an extremely wealthy donor asked him, "Father, is it possible to buy your way into heaven?"

My friend answered, "No, I don't believe that's possible—but let's give it a try anyway!"

Treasure in heaven is another of those phrases we throw around without ever stopping to define it—such as "hearing God." I've explained my desire to find out what people meant by that one. Now I wanted to know what Jesus meant when He spoke of heavenly treasure. It seems awfully important. Why didn't He spell it out better?

I sought out some of the other statements from Jesus:

"Do not store up for yourselves treasures on earth, where moths and vermin destroy, and where thieves break in and steal. But store up for yourselves treasures in heaven, where moths and vermin do not destroy, and where thieves do not break in and steal." (Matthew 6:19–20)

"But when you give a banquet, invite the poor, the crippled, the lame, the blind, and you will be blessed. Although they cannot repay you, you will be repaid at the resurrection of the righteous." (Luke 14:13–14)

"So if you have not been trustworthy in handling worldly wealth, who will trust you with true riches?" (Luke 16:11)

How does God define true riches? Paul elaborated in his letter to Timothy:

> Command them to do good, to be rich in good deeds, and to be generous and willing to share. In this way they will lay up treasure for themselves as a firm foundation for the coming age, so that they may take hold of the life that is truly life. (1 Timothy 6:18–19)

It seemed clear to me that this idea of spiritual wealth is more than just a pretty turn of phrase—it's something true and highly significant. And the idea challenged my very conception of the afterlife. I had always imagined heaven as a place where everyone was equal. I'd heard "the ground is level at the foot of the cross."

It should be in heaven too, because of grace, right? All are sinful, but all will be forgiven. Our works are "like filthy rags," according to Isaiah 64:6, and salvation is the free gift of God.

Jesus told the disciples that He would go ahead to prepare mansions for us (John 14:2). It didn't sound like there were different qualities of neighborhood.

Now I wasn't so certain about all that. If there were no distinctions past the gates of paradise, why would Jesus command, "Store up for yourselves treasures in heaven" (Matthew 6:20)? Jesus said to do this more than once. Other places in the New Testament speak of it; yet, I've never heard a sermon preached on this topic.

The idea of a kind of heavenly scorecard, registering some measurement of godliness rather than worldly achievement, was something I found shocking and provocative. To this day, I believe it's one of the great underrated mysteries of the New Testament.

With this issue in mind, I began to find additional clues. "At the renewal of all things … many who are first will be last, and many who are last will be first," Jesus teaches (Matthew 19:28, 30). When I hear this verse taught, it's always in reference to servanthood here in this world. And I'm all for that; I have a lot more to say on the topic. But I also can't escape the implication of a heavenly pecking order. What will "last" look like in heaven? What about "first"?

I have my theories. I like to think that the wealth of heaven is nothing like our earthly conception of it, that perhaps the treasure of that next world comes in the peace and joy as we see broken people made whole and Christ's kingdom finally victorious.

Perhaps our good actions on earth make us more capable of perception and appreciation of these things in heaven, so we'll be "first" in that regard. If, in this life, we've done well by "the least of these," if we've blessed others after the example of Jesus, if we've nurtured our spiritual health, then perhaps there will be levels of joy possible because of our earthly preparation. At least that's what I'd like to think.

There's a simple idea here too: *people.* I know that if, in some way, I help one soul toward a heavenly destination, surely that's an investment in heavenly treasure. I suspect there will be at least a celebratory high five at the reunion on the other side.

I've looked for analogies to help me understand these things. Randy Alcorn offers a good one in his book *The Treasure Principle.* He asks us to imagine ourselves living in 1865, as the Civil War is coming to an end. We are Southerners living in the North, planning to move back home when the war is over. But we have lots of Confederate currency. Knowing the North is certain to win, we realize the wise thing to do is cash in our Confederate dollars for US currency. Its value, after all, will endure even as the other passes away. Prudently, we'd keep a few dollars on us for short-term needs as we traveled toward our Southern home—the rest we'd exchange for the more stable currency.

That makes sense to me. This world is a confederacy that will eventually be defunct. Its coinage, bright and shining at the moment, will lose all its value. I need a bit of it in the meantime, enough for my needs—it's the "coin of the realm" here—but as I've heard it said, my hearse will have no U-Haul attached to it. I can stockpile, but to what eventual end? It makes more sense to gather spiritual wealth, which means finding ways to cash in my gold for godly things. Jesus is offering us a choice: to build our lives on stuff with a "use by" date that is fast approaching, or treasure in heaven. Perishable or eternal? Seems like an easy choice—but in reality, it's not.

There is a special relevance of all this to me. I've built a career on helping people plan their estates. I've spent years exploring creative and complex ways to help people pass on more of their accumulated wealth to their children and descendants rather than to Uncle Sam. It may not sound like a noble calling, but my job description has been to help wealthy people remain wealthy and to manage their holdings when this life is over. Because I've lived in that world of investment toward the future, what God says about it is that much more striking to me.

I came to see Jesus as an eternal version of the earthly planner that I was. Jesus pointed to how we could gather and invest eternal wealth. I decided that the whole idea of legacy planning, as pleasing and popular as it is, comes down to manipulating Confederate dollars—a doomed currency. What a sobering realization that was. We use words like *forever* in our industry, as if anything other than the souls of our clients meet that criteria. We talk about future generations that we can't even be certain will come to pass. Life, the Bible says over and over, is like a vapor: here and gone.

Even in churches, the domains of spiritual thought, we talk about stewardship of our possessions. I've heard many, many sermons on money, and rightly so. People need to know what the Bible says about it. But don't we need to think more about heavenly wealth? Am I the only one who wants more information on what it is and how we can accrue it?

As I came to these realizations, I began to look at all my earthly possessions in a new way. Cars and clothing and jewelry may not even outlive me. The most valuable of my things—land and homes—will outlive me only for a while. Until then, I hold them for God. I maintain them and honor Him with them the best I can.

Still, however, there are questions. Jesus spoke of selling it all and giving it to the poor, and I see the beauty and testimony of that. But is it God's will for everyone, or just for the one man to whom Jesus suggested it, in making a point?

Then there's the other extreme of realizing the things I have are good gifts, meant for me to enjoy—as I do believe. How much emphasis do I place on that enjoyment without becoming worldly and losing my commitment to spiritual treasure? That, of course, is what caused Jesus to instruct the rich young ruler the way He did.

I know this: the Benedictine Rule, written in the sixth century as a guide for some to live according to Jesus Christ's gospel, has helped me understand that the only truly rich people are those who are satisfied with what they have. And I can be the most satisfied when I "seek first his kingdom and his righteousness," because Jesus says that then, "all these things will be given to you as well" (Matthew 6:33).

11

The One Thing
Money Can Do

A Different Paradigm on Wealth

Money is a terrible master, but an excellent servant.

—P. T. Barnum

So, you've noticed that I think about money from time to time. I guess that makes me just like everybody else in the world.

In my case, I've had various relationships with the stuff. I spent a certain number of years in a headlong rush to build as big a pile of it as possible. Then, at a certain time, I stepped back and saw a different shade of green. I began to understand that perhaps I'd been looking in the wrong place for true wealth.

Even with a different perspective on the money, I had to admit that it remained a very important topic in life. I would value it a bit less. I would use it a bit differently. But there was no question it would continue to be a necessary and vital issue as long as I remained a resident of Earth. It's obviously necessary for support- ing my family and paying my bills.

As I've said, money is the reigning American idol. An idol is defined as anything that takes the place of God as an object of intense devotion. We've built our culture on the idea that life is about the pursuit of financial wealth, and that the good life is pos- sible by attaining enough for buying what we want. But my friend

Dick Foth is fond of saying that the two things that will be with us all our lives are relationships and money, and only one of those things will make you rich. Hmmm.

As I began to think about money and my relationship to it, I decided to get a friend's input—someone I knew would have plenty of food for thought on this particular subject. Wheelock Whitney, as you will see in subsequent chapters, was a wonderful friend and mentor in addition to being a wealthy, highly respected business leader in the Twin Cities.

I phoned his office to set up a lunch appointment, and his assistant asked for some idea of the agenda. I told her I wanted to talk about money. The line went silent for a moment before she realized that was all I was going to say. Then she confirmed the date and time, and we hung up.

Wheelock and I met for our usual fun and intensely competitive game of doubles squash, then we found a restaurant and had lunch. Wheelock studied his menu, then laid it down. "I understand the agenda of our meeting is money," he said. "Which I would interpret as being: how to take some of my money and make it yours."

I laughed and told Wheelock it actually sounded like a pretty good idea—but I'd save that one for another day. "I'm actually more interested in your perspective on money," I said. "What you think about it in general. Seeing as you have your share of it, I'm guessing you have some strong opinions on the subject."

He laughed and shook his head, as if to say, *Typical Brehm.* Then he said, "Well, in that case, we have more time than we need. Our discussion will be a brief one, since I do have a theory, and since my theory is correct." He continued, "Let me clarify that we're talking about the *commodity* of money. Money in its simplest sense, as something to exchange in trade. We can agree that nearly everyone, given the choice, would choose more money over less money. And we can bypass the discussion of economic systems, fairness and oppression, and all that, because I said our discussion would be a brief one. I take it you're interested in money in the issue of how it affects people's lives."

"Bingo."

"It certainly does that—affects people's lives. But as such, as a commodity, it's the most overrated one on the face of the earth. We all know what money can't do. It can't buy love. It can't buy happiness, though people—no matter how much they deny it—continue to believe it will. It does nothing to create self-esteem; it often does the opposite, oddly enough. Nor does it protect us from chance or create a hedge against death."

"All very true."

"But it's a little-known fact that money does provide *one* thing—one and only one. This one thing can be a wonderful blessing or a terrible curse. What it provides is: *choices*. Money buys the power to make decisions, though it doesn't buy the wisdom to make good ones. For those capable of making wise choices, it's a blessing. There comes opportunity, economic freedom, and the ability to make a useful, relevant contribution to society."

"But ..."

"But, on the other hand, for those incapable of wise choices, money ends up buying a life of self-absorption, shattered relationships, wild addictions, unfettered greed, manipulation, family trauma, and ultimate emptiness. All for the same price as what the other guy bought." He paused. "Money isn't the issue; never was. It's the choices we make with it that are paramount."

Wise words from a dear and deeply missed friend.

Who Are You Calling Greedy?

Me? You've Got to Be Kidding

◆━◆━◆

Just a little more.
—JOHN D. ROCKEFELLER
(upon being asked how much more money
he'd need before he'd have enough)

To be clever enough to get all that money,
you must be stupid enough to want it.
—G. K. CHESTERTON

Pastor and author Tim Keller says that he once planned a sermon on the seven deadly sins. His wife told him she already knew which one would attract the smallest crowd. It would be the sermon on greed. And she was right on the mark but surprised him with the reason. It wasn't because people wouldn't be willing to listen to a sermon on greed, but rather because they felt it would be irrelevant. He preached that one to a few empty seats. There was also less "buzz" about it afterward.

Keller realized that few people believe they're greedy. He has related that over the years, he's had people come to him for counseling on every imaginable sin—pride, anger, gluttony, lust. But not once has anyone come to him and told him they were struggling with greed.

I must have been thinking along those lines as I led Tuesday prayer group one week. I announced the topic of generosity, but took a sharp left and traveled deeply into the subject of greed. I think that somewhere deep down, I realized that if I'd made it known we were going to talk about greed, a lot of the people in our prayer group would have come down with the flu or realized they were too busy to attend. That wasn't a topic that resonated with them. Greed was somebody else's problem.

I even tested it out. "How many in here consider themselves greedy? Let's see a show of hands."

Nothing but faces peering at one another. *Who, me?*

So before you shake your head in derision over my friends, let me put the question to *you*, reader. Are *you* greedy?

Somebody out there must be, but it's never us. The only self-admitted greedy person I can recall offhand is Gordon Gekko, the character played by Michael Douglas in the movie *Wall Street*. In an address, the stock mogul says this: "The point is, ladies and gentleman, that greed, for lack of a better word, is good. Greed is right, greed works. Greed clarifies, cuts through, and captures the essence of the evolutionary spirit. Greed, in all of its forms—greed for life, for money, for love, knowledge—has marked the upward surge of mankind."[1]

The Gekko character is fun to boo and hiss at. But he's somebody else—he's more of a caricature who is nothing like you or me. When I ask myself the all-important question, here's what I realize: *greed* is a word I apply to anyone who is richer than me. It's like the old line about the way we drive on a highway: anyone ahead of us is driving too slow and is an idiot, and anyone trying to pass us from behind is a maniac! *Our* speed is always the correct one.

The same is true for our financial condition. Those less wealthy aren't trying hard enough. Those wealthier are greedy. So, let's shift the question to the word *rich*. Are you rich? It's a relative term, so what determines your definition? I thought it might be interesting to take the broadest scale: world population. Based on the people of this planet as they really are, what is rich and what is poor? The follow statistics might surprise you:

- The majority (70 percent) of the world's wealth is in the hands of 5 percent of its people.
- Got $2,200? If so, congratulations! You're rich. Cash assets of $2,200 per adult place a person in the top 50 percent of the world's wealthiest.
- If you earned $1,500 last year, you're actually in the top 20 percent of the world's income earners.
- If you have sufficient food, decent clothes, live in a house or apartment, and have a reasonably reliable means of transportation, you are among the top 15 percent of the world's wealthy.
- Have $68,000 in assets? You're among the richest 10 percent of the adults in the world.
- If you earn $25,000 or more annually, you are in the top 10 percent of the world's income earners.
- If you have any money saved, a hobby that requires some equipment or supplies, a variety of clothes in your closet, two cars (in any condition), and live in your own home, you are in the top 5 percent of the world's wealthy.
- If you earn more than $50,000 annually, you are in the top 1 percent of the world's income earners.
- If you have more than $500,000 in assets, you're part of the richest 1 percent of the world.[2]

I don't know about you, but these facts make me realize that not only am I financially rich—I'm *crazy* rich!

Why I am I so blind to this? Actually, Jesus gives us fair

warning. In Matthew 6:19–21, Jesus talks about money and the danger of storing up treasure on earth instead of in heaven. A few verses later, in verse 24, He clearly tells us we can't serve two masters—money and God.

But interestingly, verses 22 and 23 seem totally out of context. Jesus speaks of the eyes being the lamp to the body. And He warns us of spiritual blindness. Or is there a relationship between these ideas?

I believe money and possessions can control me in three ways. Money can provide a false sense of *security*. It seems like a solid foundation until I come to random, uncontrollable occurrences: death, divorce, addiction, and business failure. Those provide the reality that I'm not secure at all.

Money can also provide me with a false sense of *significance* as people with means are treated differently than the poor, and I can tend to be on a pedestal of sorts.

Money provides a false sense of *power* by creating a mirage of self-importance and influence. Materialism is defined as an inordinate desire or dependence upon material things. It has a unique ability to blind me from its own pervasive influence.

That's where those middle verses come in—the ones that seemed out of context at first. Money can blind me. It's interesting that I don't recall Jesus warning me about spiritual blindness regarding most sins. For example, it would be hard to be blind to committing adultery, swearing, or killing someone. Those are "glaring" sins that I couldn't avoid seeing. For example, Tim Keller is fond of saying that you don't wake up one morning and say, "Hey, you're not my wife! But with the sin of greed perhaps I do have blinders on."

Back to Jesus' admonition, "To whom much has been given, much will be expected" (Luke 12:48). It seems to me that the big questions are: How much will be expected? How much am I supposed to give? What amount would be sure to please Jesus and assure me that I'm not greedy? The church typically uses the measure of the tithe, 10 percent. The next question, of course, is whether that's gross or after-tax income. And how about net worth?

I've always given a lot of money away and consider myself equally generous with my resources and my time. But what did Jesus have to say about generosity? He seemed pretty clear in Mark's Gospel when He sat down with His disciples where the offerings in the temple were being made. The group watched the wealthy people make a big show out of their magnanimous giving. But then the "poor widow" put in two very small copper coins and Jesus told them she'd given more than anyone else. In Mark 12:44, He said, "They all gave out of their wealth; but she, out of her poverty, put in everything—all she had to live on."

That radically changes my paradigm. Jesus tells me to give *sacrificially*. Ouch. As I reflect back on my life, I can't honestly recall making a donation or commitment so large that it actually impacted my lifestyle—a gift so large, I had to make a sacrifice of something else I needed or wanted. Never can I recollect a gift that actually hurt. I give out of my wealth but not out of my poverty. And by all definitions, I am rich. And greedy. Yikes!

I have a friend who ministers to the wealthy. I asked him once about his approach. He smiled and said when it comes to money, he always tells people that when we get to heaven, God will ask only two questions: (1) "What did you decide about My son, Jesus, whom I sent?" and (2) "What did you do with all that I gave you?"

Interesting. Then I asked my friend what kind of response this got, especially from those among the wealthy leaders of the business community. He said, with a big smile, "The replies were almost always the same—I'd negotiate!"

As Tim Keller has observed the Bible never treats riches and poverty as equivalent spiritual dangers. Riches are the one to keep an eye on. After all, there are *no* words from Jesus about the difficulties of poor people trying to enter the kingdom of heaven.

If I accumulate money and go on a great buying spree, surrounding myself with more than I need, I don't make Christ look very good. Instead, I glorify things. There is a reason why Paul said, "We brought nothing into the world, and we can take nothing out of it. But if we have food and clothing, we will be content with that" (1 Timothy 6:7–8).

The next question I asked myself was this: Just how important is giving in the Scriptures compared to the other things we are called to do? I did a word search and found that the word *believe* is used 289 times; the word *pray* is used 367 times; the word *love* is used 696 times. And the word *give*? The total is 1,433 times.

So it must be pretty important.

Alienation

The World's Greatest Problem

✦

Love is the only force capable of transforming
an enemy into a friend.
—MARTIN LUTHER KING JR.

Civility is not a sign of weakness.
—JOHN F. KENNEDY

In chapter 4, I described the moment when I realized our calendar had been rebooted around Jesus and how I concluded my life should be similarly realigned.

This drove me to think of the world itself in new ways. The reason for Jesus, after all, was that God so loved *the world* (John 3:16). Why couldn't the world seem to love back? Why couldn't we love each other if a perfect God could love us weak and bungling earthlings?

Problems—so many of them. You could fill a great many books listing the problems that beset the world, but I believe the greatest of all is alienation. How many other challenges are filed under that category?

Let's consider Christianity itself. For one thousand years, there was one church. Then in 1054, the breaking away of the Eastern Orthodox Church made two denominations. The Protestant revolution came along five hundred years later, and now there were three large divisions within Christendom.

But as time went on, we really got the hang of dividing. The best guess is that we have thirty-three thousand denominations today—*exponential* division. And each division usually comes from some point of disagreement that festers and leads to alienation. Each group presumably believes it follows the real Jesus, and the other 32,999 must have it wrong. Each one, in all likelihood, has hijacked Jesus in some way and customized Him to fit its requirements.

Yet, there is essentially one Scripture. Think of it: thirty-three thousand variations on a theme. God just wanted us to know He loves us, and out of that we've made chaos, wars, and vast alienation.

Was this what Jesus intended—small groups of people who think they have it right and that everyone else must be wrong to some lesser or greater degree? Thinking that Jesus favors their particular little circle?

I don't think so. As Abraham Lincoln is reported to have wisely said, "Rather than pray that God be on our side, we need to pray that we are on His side."

The consequences of alienation in America and around the world are obvious. Our nation and the world are more divided than ever—politically, religiously, economically, and culturally. In so many ways we find ourselves at odds with our neighbors both at home and far away. But maybe we should accept it as is. Maybe things are more efficient when we divide ourselves in like-minded groups.

Why is unity worth seeking?

For me, the short answer is because God wants it. Unity pleases Him. "How good and pleasant it is when God's people live together in unity" (Psalm 133:1).

On the last night of His life on earth, Jesus prayed for unity in these words:

"My prayer is not for them alone. I pray also for those who will believe in me through their message, that all of them may be one, Father, just as you are in me and I am in you. May they also be in us so that the world may believe that you have sent me. I have given them the glory that you gave me, that they may be one as we are one—I in them and you in me—so that they may be brought to complete unity." (John 17:20–23)

And why was Jesus praying for this? In verse 24, He says unity shows the world that He was sent by God. That's a pretty significant statement. What does our disunity say? I'm addressing in this chapter the kind of unity Jesus prayed about that night.

To begin, amid all the finger-pointing and animosity in our society today, I often need to remember that those of us who follow Jesus begin with one great point of unity: we've all done things that displease God and bring shame to ourselves. Confession accomplishes nothing unless we turn away from our poor behavior (we call that *repentance*). And Jesus made it clear that for every portion of forgiveness I seek, there is a portion of forgiveness I must offer.

Satan's favorite weapons are disunity and alienation. He collects slivers of discord, distrust, misunderstanding, and envy that mount up between people and magnifies the differences. Then he uses fear, rumor, and suspicion to further divide different cultures, races, and beliefs. Has he been successful? Read a history book or look at the current headlines and you'll have your answer. (You may have some questions on this subject of the devil. We'll get to him in chapter 22.)

That's a lot of resistance against what God wants for me. So how can I go about experiencing the unity that Jesus prayed for?

First, as shown in chapter 3, I believe I must lose my religion. That is, I need to stop clutching the extraneous dogma that burdens down our relationships and creates divisions. The essentials of who Jesus is and what He wants me to do—with these alone, I can "travel light" and find more common ground with others.

I need to keep Jesus before me rather than in a box I carry. He won't accept being boxed in. He is constitutionally resistant to the various ways religions and systems would attempt to reshape and repackage Him. Remember, what the world considers wisdom is actually foolishness:

- The world looks upon the rich and declares them winners. Jesus says those the world sees as poor will inherit the kingdom of heaven.
- Our culture tells us to "find" ourselves, and we promote ourselves on Facebook. Jesus told us to die to self, because finding our lives comes only in losing them.
- Society instructs us to be self-sufficient, but Jesus requires utter dependence.
- We chase possessions, yet Jesus calls us to give them away.
- We are always seeking more blessings, but Jesus tells us to be thankful for what we have.
- We want to revenge the wrongs done to us, yet Jesus tells us to forgive.
- We are competitive, yet Jesus calls us to be compassionate.
- We judge our neighbors. Jesus tells us not to cast stones until we ourselves are free of sin.
- Our culture emphasizes personal rights. Jesus underscores duty and responsibility to others.
- The world loves money. Scripture tells us the love of money is the root of all evil.
- Our society has become addicted to security, pleasure, and ego, yet Jesus commands us to live in faith, sacrifice, and submission.

- We seek pleasure, but Jesus tells us to pick up our crosses and follow Him.

Here's just one example of my struggling with Jesus' commands. I'm to love those with whom I disagree—even my "enemies." Scripture states most clearly that loving those who love us back doesn't count. That comes naturally. But loving an enemy requires a supreme force of will and a devotion to something beyond my own self-interest.

We want a Jesus who is on our side in the issues that divide us. But we've got it backward. He calls *us* to be on *His* side. Jesus didn't say He had the truth; He said He *was* the truth! Think about that one for a minute.

So, where are the key points of disunity? Politics may be the most obvious. The United States seems more divided today than at any time in our history other than the Civil War. A member of Congress recently confided in me that the definition of a friend in Washington is someone who is willing to stab you in the chest!

John F. Kennedy wisely said, "Civility is not a sign of weakness." In political debate, why is it so difficult for us to challenge the thought rather than attacking the thinker? We should be able to disagree on policy without questioning motives.

I have experienced this kind of unity myself. In Minneapolis, we have a small group that has been meeting around Jesus every Tuesday for the last fifteen years. We come from different political parties and denominations and have widely varying views of Jesus. But we have grown to love each other not in spite of our differences but, I think, because of them.

Being a political conservative, I had always carried an unspoken assumption that liberals either lacked intelligence or they were actually out to do harm. Among the liberal members of our group are a former governor and state attorney general, as well as a well-known columnist. Over time, they forced me to reevaluate my prejudice. For I discovered they were all more intelligent than I, and we shared common ground on caring for the poor. Our differences were only in tactics and these could be discussed in ways that offered light rather than heat. We've now become the closest of friends.

Alienation is perhaps most evident in Washington, DC, where the atmosphere has become increasingly toxic and where many members of Congress won't even speak with one another. A few years ago, I was on an airplane flying from Minneapolis to Washington. I found myself seated next to one of our representatives, Betty McCollum. Betty and I had shared, along with her daughter and my son, a tremendous experience of meeting Bono when he was in Minnesota a few months previously. But at the time, we hadn't known each other well. I'd just been appointed chairman of USADF, and Betty and I had a shared passion for helping the truly poor and oppressed in Africa.

After considerable conversation, Betty turned and said, "How in the world did you get appointed to USADF by a Republican president? After all, it's a *political* appointment."

I smiled. "Well, for starters, I'm a Republican."

She nearly dropped her cup of coffee and stared at me in disbelief. "I can't believe it. You're really a Republican?"

"Yup," I replied.

"Well, Ward," she said, "you sure don't sound like a Republican. And you just don't *seem* like a Republican."

"Betty," I said, "how many have you really talked to lately?"

Betty looked across the aisle at Jim Ramstad, an eighteen-year veteran of Congress, and said somewhat wistfully, "I wish I could have been in Congress back in the 'good old days,' when people of differing opinions and parties actually talked to one another and were friends. They could remain strident and passionate opponents on issues, yet somehow the atmosphere was a cordial one. It was actually possible to 'agree to disagree.'"

Today, I think it's more common for people to seek to spend their time exclusively with people who think the same way they do. But at what cost? Huddling with the like-minded can rob us of perspective and wisdom we can't attain in any other way. Limiting my circulation to people with whom I agree is comfortable and safe, but ultimately it serves to reinforce my own ideas and prejudices. Without iron sharpening iron—the testing of opposing views—I can't grow. Neither can I know whether I'm actually right.

Not only that, but there are far more serious implications of cultural exclusivism. It's easier to resent those who are different from us and to fan the flames of anger. Countless lives have been lost in the tribal struggles between Hutus and Tutsis in central Africa, the senseless killings in the Middle East, and all the political atrocities that seem to be happening on a regular basis throughout the world.

As we see the bloodshed on our TV and computer screens, we have little doubt that unity is worth striving for.

We all know that to whom much has been given, much is expected. Jesus said it, and it's good common sense.

This makes certain demands of those of us among the affluent. But it applies to more than money; I need to be giving from my heart. I believe the current model of giving is broken. The needy and the nonprofit charities come "hat in hand" to those with resources. The affluent give with some degree of benevolence, as well as some degree of weariness that the requests only grow deeper the more we give. We wonder if we're making a difference or merely creating dependency.

What if I center my strategies on my understanding of Jesus? This would demand more of me than answering the door and putting something in the hat. I would now need to engage the needy themselves in true relationship, treating them with dignity and partnering with them to make real changes along the model that

Jesus left us. I'd be giving myself rather than simply my money. Isn't that what Jesus wants me to do?

While faith in Jesus would point us toward charity in its many forms, it's also clear that religion seems to break us apart rather than bring us together. Instead of magnifying the things that separate, I can try to build relationships and focus on the things that increase understanding and respect, such as genuine compassion and interest in others' lives.

What about those with whom I disagree? I need to do less judging and more loving. My focus should be on the fact that far, far too many have yet to hear the gospel in a compelling way. Instead, they know about our arguments. They hear mostly about the Jesus of ideological packaging, whose name is shouted in anger and whose face is painted on battle shields.

What if multitudes of people could hear, for once, about the real Jesus, the one I've at least attempted to describe in this book? My experience is that virtually everyone responds to the authentic Jesus. My belief is that the entire planet could be unified through His power and principles.

Which happens to be God's intention.

Once we were required to travel the world to see the people of the world. Now they come to us as immigrants. This causes us to reexamine yet another of Jesus' commands. He has told us to love our neighbor—defining *neighbor* as someone different than we are.

Our first impulse upon confronting difference is to react in fear or simply to turn away. Jesus won't let us off that easily; He calls us to love, and He provides no loopholes (though people have spent a great deal of time trying to locate a few). "Love your neighbor" seems like a simple platitude until we actually try to do it.

As a follower of Jesus, I need to love people of different colors, nationalities, cultures, and faiths. I need to make them feel welcome, eagerly inviting them to become a vibrant part of our society. It's an American tradition. Even as I stay committed to my personal faith journey, I need to have respect and show dignity for others in their beliefs.

It's highly significant that Jesus said the way nonbelievers would know us was by our love. Do they today? We'd rather focus on issues of truth (i.e., doctrine).

Truth without love, Scripture tells us, is like a clanging gong—so much empty noise—just as love without truth is mere sentimentality. We need both! With everything I do, I need to start at mercy, lead with love, *then* face the facts. When I start with the facts, I tend to exempt myself from extending mercy and call it love. God is love, the Bible tells us in 1 John 4:8. We're never told that He is doctrine or dogma or facts. Love should be the starting point.

Pope John Paul II put it well when he once remarked that the church can impose nothing. It can only propose, lovingly, humbly, and winsomely. In other words, we must earn the right to be heard, because people will care what we know once they know that we care. Only when people realize that we care will they allow us to become their friends, to unite with them. But first, we must put our own alienating prejudices and assumptions away.

In 1994, I was invited to my first National Prayer Breakfast in Washington, DC, by Senator Dave Durenberger, who'd become a very close friend. The evening before the Breakfast, Senator Durenberger and I attended the United Nations dinner, which he was hosting. I glanced at the table next to mine, and sitting there was Ayatollah Sayyid Ali Khamenei, the Supreme Leader, from Iran.

I have to be honest in saying that the first thought that crossed my mind was, *What is* he *doing here?* But a more logical question replaced that emotional one: What was *he* doing at a prayer breakfast based on the principles and precepts of Jesus? It was a nearly surreal moment.

The dinner included many speakers, all of them offering different perspectives of Jesus. We heard fascinating stories of the impact of Jesus all around the world. My thoughts occasionally strayed to that nearby table, and I wondered, *What does he think of that?*

Toward the end of the evening, Senator Durenberger acknowledged the Ayatollah's presence, and he offered the distinguished Muslim leader a chance to speak. It became clear that many in the room hadn't realized with whom they were dining—a number of them stood and walked out. Just as bad, I could hear the whispers: "He has nothing to say to me!"

I knew I was in for something interesting. But what?

The aging Ayatollah was in a wheelchair, escorted by his son. He began by telling Senator Durenberger that he was both surprised and honored to be asked to speak. He spoke very softly and then said that, while the world and religion tend to emphasize all of the differences we have about Jesus, they seldom, if ever, talk about the similarities. He went on to say that Muslims believe that Jesus was of a virgin birth, is the most revered prophet in Islam, and will someday return to redeem the world. All of this was news to me! Then he paused, the room dead quiet, before saying he wanted to share one thing he knew for sure: if Abraham, Moses, and Jesus were all walking and talking together on the earth today, their biggest question would be, "Why is all this killing in the world being done in our names?"

When I reflect on the Ayatollah's words and acknowledge that Jesus devoted many of His last moments on earth praying for unity, I realize it's something I need to take seriously.

On This Rock

Thoughts on the Church and Hypocrisy

The church is a hospital for sinners, not a museum for saints.

—Saint Augustine

I do not reject your Christ. I love your Christ.
It's just that so many of you Christians
are so unlike your Christ.

—Mahatma Ghandi

To summarize my thoughts in the past few pages, alienation is the question and Jesus is the answer. But in thinking about both those subjects, we continually find ourselves crossing over into the issue of the church. It stands poised between the problem that is isolation and the solution that is Jesus. Or it should.

As I thought about what matters in life, I had to consider what matters for the church. I went back to what I considered the first occasion when the subject was broached: Jesus telling Peter that "on this rock I will build my church, and the gates of Hades will not overcome it" (Matthew 16:18).

In case you're not familiar with that verse, Jesus was giving His disciple Simon a new name, Peter, which in Greek means "rock." And He made a little play on words in describing what He would build upon that rock.

In Matthew 7:24–27, Jesus also offered a parable in which a man builds a sturdy house upon a rock rather than sand. The "sand house," of course, is toppled during the first bout with bad weather. But the winds and the storm beat upon the "rock house" in vain. Similarly, the forces of hell would fail to topple the "house" that Jesus built, as He told Peter.

But we're left with the question of what Jesus actually meant when He used the word *church*. We've defined it in all kinds of ways, but if we could only get through to the precise idea He imagined, we'd have the model for the most perfect church there could be.

I think of those lovely huge cathedrals in Europe that stand as lonely testaments to what happens when the building trumps the Builder. Centuries of physical storms haven't toppled those great churches, but apathy has emptied them. They're grand and inspiring outside but cold and dark within. On that continent, many people have chosen the ways of the world over tired homilies, rigid doctrine, and limp prayers.

Judgment has its place, and the words of Jesus made that perfectly clear. But when lifeless doctrine overshadows His good news of grace and love, a church of personal healing, worship, and reflection can quickly become a valley of dry bones. Ezekiel, the Old Testament prophet, walked through a graveyard of battle and God asked him, "Son of man, can these bones live?" (Ezekiel 37:3).

God takes us among dead and dying churches and asks us the same question. If the bones are to rise from the dust, the church must resume providing compelling answers to spiritual questions, longings, and needs.

But some would say there's a deeper problem than what the church isn't doing—it's what the church *has* done, often tragically. Critics rightfully point to the bloody exploits of the Crusades, various inquisitions to "purify" the church by way of torture, and untold deaths in wars over belief differences.

In modern times, we've seen the tragic stories of fallen TV evangelists and serial child abuse covered up by high-ranking church officials. Best-selling books advocating atheism make the case that virtually every human failing can somehow be placed at the feet of religious belief. Whether that allegation is true, what can never be denied is that neither Jesus nor His teachings are responsible for any of those things. The problems come from damaged people who twist the faith for their own purposes.

And yes, the church is indeed home to plenty of hypocrites, as skeptics love to point out. You'll find no shortage of them, but nothing about Jesus produces or supports hypocrisy. In fact, hypocrisy was the one thing that truly seemed to anger Him. Jesus saw the needy masses as little children, innocent and gullible. He said those who would lead astray these "little ones" would be better off to have great millstones tied around their necks and thrown into the sea (Matthew 18:6). He overturned tables at the courts of the temple when He saw profiteering taking over holy ground— the one place people could come to experience the presence of God (21:12). He called the religious leaders "whitewashed tombs" (23:27) and a "brood of vipers" (v. 33). He was angry on behalf of the helpless people He loved, the people who were under the spiritual care of those same religious leaders.

Pretty stern stuff, huh? There was no "meek and mild" Jesus when it came to hypocrisy. My theory is that Jesus was infuriated most by the harm hypocrisy does to the people who come to Him or to spiritual leaders for help. False steps of hypocrisy by the church, large and small, undermine any quantity of good work the church might do.

Richard Rohr, a Franciscan priest, succinctly summarizes some of the challenges organized religion faces when it gets off track from the principles and precepts of Jesus. He believes the major cause of atheism is the hypocritical cheap grace being offered to people today in the name of spirituality. In any case, people believe that after centuries of time, religious belief should show some evidence of changed lives. Sadly, any changes people do see are often for the worse. "I wish I did not have to say this,"

Rohr writes, "but religion either produces the very best people or the very worst."[1] In fact, Jesus makes this very point quite often in the Gospels. When there's nothing more than a belief system or a code of behavior, the result is divisions among people, "whereas actual faith puts all our parts (body, heart, and head) on notice and on call."[2] The true essence of conversion is to put aside all the superfluous religious add-ons and get to what Jesus has placed right in front of us: the simple essence of gospel life. It seems so simple, but in reality, it's often complicated.

I'll admit I've been tempted to reject the church in frustration, but I've also realized I must distinguish between what Jesus actually told me to do and the interpretation of those instructions by various religious groups—or by any of the well-intentioned among us who might superimpose our desires and ideas on the teachings of Jesus.

Still, I've also realized nothing has really changed; I imagine that Jesus' anger burns even today. I can almost see Jesus walking through the places where young children are abused and through the motels where prominent pastors are caught up in sordid affairs, overturning more tables. Perhaps He overturns the pulpits of ministers railing against homosexuality while guarding their own dark secrets. Maybe He walks into the mailrooms where large staffs shake money out of letters, offered by desperately poor people so their beloved TV preacher can buy a nicer jet. I have days when I wonder if Jesus wishes to overturn the church itself and start over, as in the days of Noah.

Then I read what I've just written, or tune in to my own thoughts, and hear the tones of self-righteousness, the easy finger-pointing. Am I one to judge? I read the story in John 8:3–11, in which the woman is caught in adultery and the crowd gathers, armed with rocks and ready to fire away. I'd like to think I would have helped protect the woman as Jesus did. But I can't be certain—not knowing my own moral weakness.

My friend Rick Warren has two items that provide him with a tangible means to remember not to judge others. The first is a large rock that sits on his desk and says, "Let he without sin cast the first stone." The second is a miniature tape measure Rick keeps in his pocket at all times. On it is engraved these words from Matthew 7:2: "With the measure you use, it will be measured to you."

It's such a slippery slope that leads from righteous anger to self-righteous hypocrisy; it's yet another spiritual trap. Becoming angry at the things that make Jesus angry is right, as long as I don't think myself superior. Once I hear the words "I could never do something like that," I know I've lost my way.

There was an occasion when a prominent member of Twin City society was publicly exposed in a sordid tale of adultery. The inevitable round of self-satisfied gossip and tongue wagging ensued, and I found myself unintentionally shaking a finger of indictment as I talked about it with my business partner. He listened quietly.

When there was a pause in the conversation, he said, "There but for the grace of God go I." That old saying is often attributed to John Bradford, an English evangelical preacher from the 1500s. According to legend, he would stand at his window and watch prisoners led to their hanging. "There but for the grace of God goes John Bradford," he would murmur. I believe he was onto something.

The failure of another man doesn't heighten my own righteousness; it only reminds me of my own spiritual brittleness. And sure enough, when I take a long, deep look into the very private depths of my own heart, unvarnished by rationalizations and excuses, I find I no longer have the urge to cast a stone at some fellow struggler of presumably more sinful pedigree.

This is, I believe, the only true antidote for the poison of hypocrisy: the humility that comes from deep soul-searching and honest self-evaluation. I have to rid myself of any faith in my own ability to please God. Apart from Jesus, I'm utterly without hope. As I see it, then, the church is about people coming together in the loneliness that comes from that self-realization. We all need God. We all need one another. God made us part of one church, though we keep finding ways to divide off into new cliques and splinter groups—yet God will not acknowledge our little walls, boundaries, and fiefdoms. He is eternally, patiently about reconciliation rather than alienation.

For example, what I call the Old Testament and my Jewish friends the Torah is part of an amazing mosaic of the presence of God among us. My Jewish friends are still my family. Jesus never declared a new denomination or schism. He never turned from His Jewish heritage. He was a rabbi and died as one. It was at the Council of Jerusalem or Apostolic Council test held in Jerusalem around 50 AD where Christians began drawing distinctions. Passover and other rich traditions, steeped in Scripture, were cast aside as a result. Our reading of the Torah is all the poorer because of that.

As a Christian church, we made it one thousand years before we found occasion to divide off: Catholic and Eastern Orthodox. Then it was half that time, about five hundred years, before the Western church divided into Catholic and Protestant. From there, we found it easier and easier to spin off new variations on the basic theme Jesus had set forth—the simple gospel. Isn't the irony rich and tragic? Jesus came to make us one, and we use Him to find new ways to divide. Therefore, I can't help but read the life and words of Jesus and draw a conclusion about what He meant when He talked about building His church on that rock. I don't believe He was talking about dogma and doctrine. He spent none of His time laying that out in His teachings. Instead, I believe He meant He was building a fellowship, a gathering of people who would make a covenant to live and love in close relationship. The picture of that is found in the book of Acts. It's apparent to me that the first generation of Jesus followers believed what Jesus said and lived out what He taught. Can we rediscover that formula in the twenty-first century?

The Quaker theologian Elton Trueblood commented that Jesus perpetuated His life and teaching by laying the foundations of a redemptive society. He formed none of the usual organizational structures and wrote no handbooks. Instead, He collected a handful of unpromising men and women and tasked them with creating a new society such as the world had never seen. Jesus took this quite seriously, going so far as to call this new society a "town built on a hill" (Matthew 5:14) and the "salt of the earth" (v. 13), insisting that if the salt should fail, so would the world—for the salt is the only preservative. The church, therefore, isn't an alternative philosophy but the only hope for humanity. We need to be set on that hill, where people look up to us and hope, rather than looking down upon us in disappointment.

Trueblood concludes that we have all our emphases in the wrong places. We don't need theories or even preaching so much as a demonstration:

> There is only one way of turning people's loyalty to Jesus, and that is by loving others with the great love of God. We cannot revive faith by argument, but we might catch the imagination of puzzled men and women by an exhibition of a fellowship so intensely alive that every thoughtful person would be forced to respect it. If there should emerge in our day such a fellowship, wholly without artificiality and free from the dead hand of the past, it would be an exciting event of momentous importance. ... A wise person would travel any distance to join it.[3]

Jesus meant the church to be anything but boring. If it had been so dull and tame from the beginning, nobody would have been martyred. Christians would have been considered too harmless, and the movement would have died off soon enough. The church came alive through the great mystery and power of the Holy Spirit, who will never allow boredom. The fellowship was made up of common folks who fished or farmed for a living, doctors and scholars, once-corrupt tax collectors and ex-prostitutes—people from every layer of society, people with nothing in common but their love for and reliance upon Jesus, people who (like all people) were hypocrites looking to end their alienation. They set the world on fire, and they did it completely without the assistance of megachurches and multimillion-dollar communications ministries. Their model indicates to me that larger isn't better. Rather, close, intimate sharing among smaller circles of folks who know and care for one another is the key for living out the teachings of Jesus. And as Trueblood has written, if we will just do that, people will knock down the doors to get in.

As modern churches inevitably become "mega" in a crowded urban world, many larger churches promote small groups who gather together apart from Sunday services to better share more intimately their questions, concerns, trials, and lives. Rick Warren is encouraged by the fact that there are more people attending small groups within Saddleback Church than the forty thousand or so who actually attend Sunday services. What makes it all go is the excitement of true intimacy as people come together to follow Jesus and become the new creations He has made them.

It seems logical, then, to define the church not based upon specific brick-and-mortar buildings but on the spiritual blueprint in the mind of Jesus when He changed the name of a fisherman once known as Simon. What is that blueprint? Perhaps it's laid out after all in physical form in Acts 2:42–47:

> They devoted themselves to the apostles' teaching and to fellowship, to the breaking of bread and to prayer. Everyone was filled with awe at the many wonders and signs

performed by the apostles. All the believers were together and had everything in common. They sold property and possessions to give to anyone who had need. Every day they continued to meet together in the temple courts. They broke bread in their homes and ate together with glad and sincere hearts, praising God and enjoying the favor of all the people. And the Lord added to their number daily those who were being saved.

Alienation is the problem, and Jesus is the solution. And while the church is imperfect and is made up of imperfect (hypocritical) people, it draws people together so they can better focus on Jesus. Jesus called the church His bride. When I think of it that way, it becomes the precious and invaluable institution as He imagined it.

15

Calling Each Other's Cards

The Thing Everyone Needs but No One Wants

When a man points a finger at someone else,
he should remember that four of his fingers
are pointing at himself.

—Louis Nizer

When it comes to privacy and accountability,
people always demand the former for themselves
and the latter for everyone else.

—David Brin

Doug Coe is the most famous person you've never heard of. George H. W. Bush said this about him: "Doug Coe has more friends who are heads of state than I do."

Doug died just a few days before I started writing this book and had been a great mentor in my life. He knew his parables as well as his politics. He was comfortable with the man on the street as much as he was with the numerous heads of state he befriended and counseled. And somewhere down the long list of his accomplishments was his willingness to be my mentor. I used to be extremely proud of this until I realized there were literally thousands of others he took under his wing.

Doug was on his way to the Twin Cities after a particularly

hectic round of traveling. Being responsible for his itinerary in Minneapolis, I decided what he probably needed most was an opportunity simply to stop and catch his breath. So why not a round of golf and an afternoon to hang out?

We got to the golf course, and, between holes, Doug brought up a subject I didn't anticipate. "Ward, one thing I really believe in is the place of the small prayer group—just a small of band of brothers who meet to pray for each other and hold each other accountable. Is there a group like that in your life?"

"I haven't found a good one," I said.

"Hmmm. Well, let me share something with you. What if I told you'd I'd been praying for ten years that such a group of leaders would come together here in Minneapolis?"

His revelation caught me by surprise. "That's very interesting, Doug. How did you come to pray for something like that?"

"Well, I see more and more that if God is going to do something in an area, it usually starts with a few guys committed to praying together. I'm talking about no more than twelve men—leaders, but laity. No ministers. And it shouldn't be built around one strong personality who leads. Leadership rotates each week. Ward, are you familiar with the end portion of the second chapter of Acts?"

"Yes, it's a terrific passage."

"In verse 42, it talks about how the first disciples devoted themselves to the apostles' teaching and to fellowship, to the breaking of bread and to prayer. Incredible things came out of that. And they still do."

Doug went on to surprise me by sharing about how nonpartisan groups were meeting on that basis in the US Senate every Wednesday. That certainly caught my attention, given my view that Capitol Hill was the most partisan place on earth.

But the movement was also spreading all across the world, from Oslo to Entebbe, from Tokyo to Berlin, from Sydney to San Francisco. In this complex world, men were getting back to basics, meeting in small groups where they could pray and share their lives and talk about the teachings of Jesus.

It was all fascinating and inspiring, until we put up our golf clubs, at which time I forgot all about it.

But on the previous day, I'd gotten a call from my friend Wheelock Whitney. Wheelock had heard I was hosting Doug Coe, and he wanted in. So, he was calling to remind me of all the nice things he'd done for me, including inviting me to Augusta National Golf Club to play golf on the site of the Masters Tournament. He was calling in his marker.

Why? Because Wheelock had heard a lot about Doug, particularly through mutual friends, including Senator Harold Hughes. Wheelock had wanted to get to know Doug for a long time.

It wasn't that I wanted Doug all to myself; the problem was, he would be in and out of town all day. He was to make one stop to speak at a dinner at my church, but Wheelock had to be somewhere else about that time. He kept pressing, and then I had a brainstorm. Wheelock could drive us to church, they could talk in the car, and then Doug and I would catch a ride home with my wife, Kris.

Not surprisingly, Doug and Wheelock hit it off immediately. The conversation flowed as we drove, and I enjoyed just listening in like a fly on the wall. Here were two of my coveted mentors, who had before never met, becoming friends. They exchanged a hug as we were dropped off, and they promised to renew their acquaintance in the future. We turned to walk into the church.

Doug turned to me and said, "Ward, that's the guy."

"Okay. What guy?"

"The small group, Ward, the small group. He's the nucleus. Ask him."

"Now wait a minute, Doug. Wheelock is one of the busiest men in this state, and I don't really know him well enough to ask him something like that. Shouldn't it come from you?"

"Nope. Your job." He smiled, and that was that.

After that moment, I thought about it. Maybe I prayed about it. But I had my doubts. For me, Wheelock was a guy to play doubles squash with, every morning at eleven. That group didn't get any closer to religion than the swear words that were issued after bad shots.

Doug knew he had planted a seed that would take root inside me, grow, and worry me half to death. Just as it did. I made every attempt simply to dismiss it from my mind, but it wouldn't go away.

I didn't want to do what Doug had asked. But I didn't like feeling guilty over it either. So, I figured I'd ask Wheelock the big question and get it over with. And if Wheelock laughed at me, so be it. I called Wheelock's office. And to my disappointment, he happened to be available. His assistant put him on the line, and I said, "Hello, Wheelock, I have an issue to discuss."

"Discuss it, then."

"Well, I'd rather not do it on the phone. Could I stop by your office sometime?"

"Sure. All you have to do is walk upstairs."

We were in the same building. There was no place for me to hide. I went into his office and stammered through my explanation of Doug's small group idea. I don't know how lucid I was, but Wheelock watched me carefully.

After I finished, he said, "Ward, I'm not exactly sure what you're asking me here. And frankly, you're not doing a very good job asking it."

"I know," I said, sighing and looking at my hands.

"Are you asking me if I'd be interested in starting a small group? I would assume to meet together regularly—though you didn't say whether it would be daily, weekly, or monthly. And maybe for breakfast, prayer together, Bible study, and fellowship, whatever that means—is that what you're asking me?"

"Yes. That's the gist of it."

"Well, Ward, I want you to know I've been waiting for *ten years* for someone to ask me that."

For ten years, Doug had been praying for a guy like Wheelock, and Wheelock had been waiting for a catalyst like Doug. Somehow, I was the strange little cog missing from the machine!

Doug had been clear on certain things: no leader but Jesus. No denominations or doctrinal distinctions. From there, just follow Acts 2:42.

We did our best to do that. New members were added slowly and by unanimous agreement only. We knew that getting people in was easy; asking them to leave, a nightmare. So, we were deliberate in building the group. Still, within the year, we had a former senator, a former governor, a state attorney general, a newspaper columnist, a former professional basketball star, and the rest were leaders in business. By design, the group covers the full political spectrum, and we do discuss those issues—respectfully and with the aim of generating light rather than heat. Seventeen years have come and gone, and I imagine we'll keep meeting as long as Tuesdays keep coming.

For me, the most amazing thing has been the big picture I've been allowed to take in. In my travels, I've seen and sat in small groups like ours in Kenya, Burundi, Rwanda, Eastern Congo, Uganda, Ethiopia, Liberia, and Ghana. I can only conclude that Doug was right—all across the world, God is doing a big thing from many "small packages."

One of the most intriguing stories I heard was of the group founded in Japan. Some of their political leaders had been invited to the National Prayer Breakfast and learned about this movement of Jesus-based small groups. Their religious background was Shinto, and they knew nothing of this Jesus of Nazareth. But they were intrigued and wanted to learn more about Him. Now, at the National Prayer Breakfast, they'd heard that Jesus told us to love our enemies. To these folks, this was a brand-new concept.

The Japanese leaders went home and started their own gathering. They called their group, Love Your Enemy, and it was something of a bold experiment. Members of opposing political parties, who might be considered enemies themselves, sat in the same room. They weren't going to stop at having a scriptural discussion; they were going to try things out. The week's assignment was literally to go out of the room and love an enemy.

The stories that came back were startling and moving. That group lives on, taking the words of Jesus and trying them on for size. As far as I know, every teaching has worked, as people have found to be true for two thousand years.

Back in Minneapolis, our Tuesday gathering has become a large fixture in our lives. Attendance is mandatory if members are in town and in good health, so it can't be scheduled over. That hasn't been a temptation as we've seen what the group is all about. We take turns leading each week, announcing a topic in advance and a passage to read.

For fifteen to twenty minutes, the leader shares his thoughts about the topic, then we take turns sharing our insights and questions around the table. There's full confidentiality—what's said in Tuesday group stays in Tuesday group—and thus the meeting often becomes a support group for someone who reaches out. We all live our lives knowing that whatever happens, the group is there for us, and we share one another's burdens.

Jesus has made this promise: when two or more gather in His name, He will show up. We save Him a seat, and He hasn't missed a meeting yet. From week to week I have a sense that such a meeting "is good and pleasing to God" (1 Timothy 2:3). The band of brothers is a rare and valuable thing—a safe place for any subject to be discussed, for disagreeing yet loving each other no less. Only the expression of anger is off-limits. Tears may come, and this is one assembly of guys that can handle them. Men discover they can take off their masks and be real, with no negative consequences. Transparency is achieved with a great sense of liberation.

In other settings, I find men hesitant to share with a single other person, let alone a group. Sure, bantering about sports, politics, and the stock market is safe, but guys won't open up about the things in life that really matter. The world has taught them they need to be strong and independent—Marlboro men who, at all costs, won't show any sign of "weakness."

The problem is that this isn't God's agenda. He didn't design us to be mask wearers who broadcast a strength and independence we don't possess. The fact is we're human, we have weaknesses, and we need each other.

We need one other thing too—accountability. Who holds us accountable in all the areas of life where we take the lead? I find this word to be the most overtalked and seldom practiced discipline in all the body of Jesus' teachings. We're all alike in needing it desperately and not wanting it just as desperately.

I need accountability because I'm personally capable of rationalizing almost any questionable behavior in my life. Over the past few years, I've become painfully aware of that fact. I do a predictably good job of looking at others with a critical eye and seeing *their* flaws. With myself (the only one I'm actually responsible for), it's a different matter.

Rick Warren defines rationalization as "rational lies." I can allow myself to do something I'd harshly judge the other guy for doing. Then, if Kris or someone else asks what I was thinking, the answer is usually that I *wasn't* thinking. That's the whole problem. I find it as fascinating as it is depressing. Also, the more I commit a sin, the less it seems like one. The easier the rationalization, the worse I become. What a mess.

All of that is why I need someone to hold me accountable. To put it in the language of Jesus, I need someone to help me realize there's a beam in my eye; thus, I have no time for the speck in someone else's eye. But who will I actually listen to while they're trying to help me with something that can sting?

The answer came in the form of a great gift. I was attending a faith-based gathering of business types with a friend named Rich when the facilitator brought up the need for accountability. It wasn't the first time. In fact, I think most followers of Jesus understand the *need* for accountability—they just don't want to *have* it.

As I thought about the words being said, and then about Rich, the managing partner and world-class litigator in an international law firm, I thought, *He might be the guy.*

I'd definitely need someone tough and direct enough to "call my cards." Rich was. I asked him if he wanted to give the accountability thing a go, and he agreed.

It was both difficult and awkward. We decided to wade gently into it and started our weekly phone call "check-ins," talking mostly about our faith and prayer. Having granted each other authority, it has now evolved into our speaking truth into each other's finances, marriages, relationships with our kids—our entire lives.

The first time Rich was able to show me where I was going badly wrong, it felt like an unexpected rebuke, and my knee-jerk reaction was to be highly defensive. Then I realized the only possible agenda he could have was our agreement to speak with authority into one another's lives, as well as genuine concern and caring for me.

As the dated saying goes, "Only your best friend will tell you that you throw a ball like a girl." So true. In virtually all of our human interaction, we're long on compliments and encouragement but hesitant to bring up anything that might offend, regardless of how obvious it may be.

That was a game changer. Over time, a deep trust has developed and nothing is off the agenda. I've been deeply blessed by both the very personal one-on-one accountability with Rich and the friendships and fellowship from the band of brothers that gathers each Tuesday.

Both involve a long history of trust. Indeed, iron sharpens iron, as Scripture tell us in Proverbs 27:17. Accountability is a gift that leads to other gifts, all of which are priceless.

16

Something about That Name

The Power of the Name Above All Names

> For to us a child is born, to us a son is given,
> and the government shall be upon his shoulders.
> And he will be called Wonderful Counselor, Mighty God,
> Everlasting Father, Prince of Peace.
> —Isaiah 9:6

> There are two hundred and fifty-six names given in the Bible
> for Jesus Christ, and I suppose this was because He was
> infinitely beyond all that any one name could express.
> —Billy Sunday

Throughout this book, I've drawn a distinction between Jesus and Christianity. Jesus is not guilty of the actions of imperfect people through the years. But I can imagine someone's objection: "Not so fast—aren't you splitting hairs? Don't you have to own both sides of the coin?"

I would reply that I've borne witness to the reality of that distinction, and it's been one of my life's richest blessings. It's not two sides of a coin; it's two separate coins. One of them is often counterfeit.

The group that meets in the US Senate and House of Representatives privately on Wednesdays in the Senate and Thursdays in the House to pray puts aside partisan agendas. Power plays are checked at the door. Political parties, religions, and denominations never get in the way of prayer and fellowship.

These friendships help initiate friendship and trust outside the boundaries of politics. If Republicans and Democrats in America could do it, why not Hutus and Tutsis in Africa?

So, in 1998, a few years following my first National Prayer Breakfast, I traveled to Kigali, Rwanda, with Senator Dave Durenberger. Our purpose was to encourage the members of the Rwandan General Assembly to form a little group, including members both Hutu and Tutsi, to meet together on a regular basis to pray for themselves and their country.

Senator Durenberger and I arranged to meet President Paul Kagame of Rwanda, on the morning of his inauguration. This man was a fierce freedom fighter and patriot who fought at the side of General Yoweri Museveni to free Uganda from the tyranny of Milton Obote. As a general, Kagame, along with his Rwandan Patriotic Front, had finally ended the genocide that claimed at least eight hundred thousand lives in that country. But now would come the hard part: the formidable task of rebuilding a country from the rubble and emotional devastation Rwanda had suffered.

When President Kagame entered the room to meet with Senator Durenberger and me, I was surprised and even a little disappointed. I had expected a Che Guevara type, a larger-than-life military general with rows of bullets crisscrossing his chest. Instead, here was a soft-spoken gentleman, tall and slender, in a fine business suit.

We discussed the economy and the huge challenges facing a government. The nation's treasury had been looted and virtually all its infrastructure lay in ruins. President Kagame shared those challenges in light of an inconvenient truth: While the world is quick to provide relief for natural disasters, it has the tendency to look the other way in the case of political genocide. Such cases are ugly and distasteful to the aid community, so funds collect at a far slower pace.

We understood the truth of his words. During a pause in the conversation, I asked the president, "What role do you see for the church in the healing and reconciliation of your country?"

And now I saw something of the warrior come to the surface—the commander rather than the statesman. President Kagame's eyes blazed and his features tightened. He leaned across the table and all but shouted, "None!"

We were taken aback.

"The church was *complicit* in the genocide," he continued. "It failed this nation completely."

I must have been ready to reply, for Dave offered me a gentle kick under the table and shifted the topic to less contentious grounds. We talked about broader socioeconomic concerns.

But soon there was another empty space in the conversation. I dared to ask the following question: "Mr. President, do you think there might be a role for Jesus in the rebuilding of Rwanda?" Immediately my shin took another hit, this one a good deal sharper. My senator friend wasn't happy with me.

But an amazing thing happened. The military side of the president faded once again, and in his place we saw a friend, a smiling man with a twinkle in his eye. He said, "Of *course* there's a role for Jesus. If my people had been following Jesus, the genocide would never have taken place."

Jesus outside the box.

Later, in 2008, I had the opportunity to travel to the Islamic Republic of Mauritania as chairman of USADF. I was there to sign a letter of understanding with the president to open a program whereby USADF would help fund enterprises and farmer co-ops.

We were scheduled to meet with the president of the country at that time, Sidi Mohamed Ould Cheikh Abdallahi. One of my friends, Senator Jim Inhofe, who was leading a congressional delegation, had visited Mauritania six months before. The group of senators met privately with the president to build a friendship based on the principles and precepts of Jesus, and they'd prayed together. As I was now heading there, I was asked to greet them and hopefully build on the relationship they'd established.

The protocol officer provided me with the logistics of the meeting. There would be television cameras and a large group of ministers and public officials, in addition to our USADF group. I asked if it might be possible to have a few minutes alone with the president following the meeting, away from the cameras and commotion.

"Impossible," the officer replied. "It's just not going to happen."

I was a little disappointed, but the meeting went on as planned. We had a pleasant diplomatic exchange about the partnership between Mauritania and USADF. Of course, it seemed a bit stiff and formal, as such gatherings do, particularly when they're being filmed. Within fifteen minutes we concluded our official business. At that point, instead of promptly leaving, the president turned to his chief of staff and said, "I'd like to have a few minutes alone with the chairman."

Eyebrows were raised around the room, including those of my new friend, Ambassador Mark Boulware. Through his own translator, the president had asked for Ambassador Boulware to remain and translate from English. The room began to clear, and I tried to consider what I was going to say. The best way I knew to do that was to ask God, so I prayed silently until the president turned and asked, very brusquely, "So, what do you want?"

We spoke through the filters of our translators. I quickly told the president I wanted nothing. I merely wished to greet him on behalf of Senator Inhofe and the small prayer group that meets in the US Senate on Wednesdays. "Ever since the senator's visit," I explained, "the group has been praying for you and for your nation."

Once again, I saw a different demeanor supplant the formal,

businesslike one. A great smile broke the surface, and the president asked me to return his greetings and wishes to "Senator Jim" and the president's new friends in Washington. It was clear that the president respected the American politician. There had been a remarkable meeting between the two, he told me, and they'd come away not as diplomats but as "brothers" (that was the word he used). The president wanted to be sure I greeted his friend.

A little less brusquely, but again with a bit of formality, the president asked, "Is that all?" Encouraged, I risked my aching shin one more time (this time by a US ambassador) by naming the name. I told the president I would love to talk for a few minutes about Jesus.

Remember, translators were involved. The ambassador, my spokesman, looked from me to the waiting face of President Abdallahi. He wasn't sure what to do—after all, we were in the *Islamic* Republic of Mauritania.

Finally, with some reluctance, Ambassador Boulware relayed my words to the president. Now there was a sea change in atmosphere. The president leaned back in his chair, no longer seeming to be doing the work of state but engaging in personal pleasure. With great enthusiasm he replied, "I can't think of anything more that I'd rather talk about than Jesus!"

Now we were speaking from the heart. A connection had been made. The president told me that he'd always been puzzled by the fact that when Muslims and Christians speak of Jesus, they focus on differences rather than what they hold in common. He wanted me to know that he loves Jesus; that his Muslim tradition holds Jesus in a special place, and Westerners need to know it; that Jesus, Muslims affirm, will return from heaven, unlike Muhammad; and that many of his friends believe in the virgin birth and in Jesus' status as the most highly revered prophet.

Not that he was ignoring the points of divergence. The major point of difference, he said, was in the doctrine of the Trinity, which Muslims cannot accept due to their understanding of the meaning of "one God." Still, the spirit of the moment was a positive and even loving one, a tender exchange that was closed by heartfelt prayer—the president, the ambassador, and myself standing and holding hands as we bowed.

Jesus outside the box.

I've found that naming the name has a peculiar power. It always gets a reaction—sometimes positive, sometimes negative, always heartfelt. The name of Jesus won't let us sit on the fence.

In our society, there's no problem in discussing "spirituality." That's in the category of acceptable sentiment, along the lines of love and kindness and a good deed for the day. People will talk about their spirituality. Even the name of God can be invoked without much fuss, because wiggle room can be found in the concept and its definition. It's understood these days that everyone gets to customize their idea of God—anything from the grandfatherly figure in a robe to a vague cosmic entity found in nature.

But mention the name of Jesus and watch what happens. The New Testament draws attention not just to Jesus but to the power of His name. In the early church, as recorded in Acts 4:10, people were healed "by the name of Jesus," and Philippians 2:10 tells us that at the name of Jesus, "every knee will bow" someday.

There is always a reaction to the spoken name. I notice that Jesus said He would draw all people to Himself (John 12:32). Notice He said that He would do the attracting and it would be for *all* people. There is a power there not our own, and it applies to everyone, no matter how far away we travel.

I've played a lot of squash with friends. On the court, too, the name of Jesus is invoked, but with no sense of reverence at all nor with any particular reaction from others. There it carries the connotation, "I made a bad shot!" As long as it's used as an expletive, the name of Jesus is no more potent than any of thousands of words in the English vocabulary.

You've noticed by now that I'm willing to drop certain questions in any situation. On the squash court, I began asking about the relationship between the name of Jesus and the racket sport. "Why not shout out 'Winston Churchill'?" I asked. "Why not 'Abraham Lincoln'? Why 'Jesus Christ'?"

The most frequent reply was, "I'm sorry, I forgot you're religious."

"No, it's not that," I'd say, half-truthfully. "I'm just curious. Why not some other name?"

There would be a moment of thought, then, "I guess there's just something about *that* name."

I suspect the "something" has to do with "that name" being the most prominent in the history of the human race. Those who are startled, angry, or in panic shout the name of Jesus or God as a reflexive action. Why? They may have no spiritual beliefs at all, but they're acknowledging, in that moment, the power of the name that is above all names.

Again, the Bible tells us that "God exalted him [Jesus] to the highest place, and gave him the name that is above every name" (Philippians 2:9). It seems to me that not all people realize that, but all people sense it.

Cold religious dogma carries no power. That isn't the power of God, but mere human descriptions of it. The names of God and the name of Jesus in particular, however, carry power. Jesus said that where two or more gather "*in my name*" (Matthew 18:20), He will be present. "Spirituality" won't accomplish that. The idea of "God, however you conceive Him" offends no one and helps no one.

But across the world, the name of Jesus is recognized for the power it bears, and I believe that someday every knee will indeed bow.

17

How Can I Love God?

Let Alone with All My Heart, Soul, Mind, and Strength

◆━◆━◆

"Love the Lord your God with all your heart and with all your
soul and with all your mind and with all your strength."
—MARK 12:30

I have a Hindu friend. We've talked about many subjects, and over the space of those conversations, matters of faith have naturally come up. He knew I had seriously changed my approach to life after I went to Africa the first time, and my remarks about Jesus had aroused his interest. He wanted to know more about Him.

I gave him the advice that made the most sense to me. "There's no need to rely on my opinions," I said. "For that matter, I wouldn't depend on any books or Bible studies. I would say the best strategy would be to get to know Jesus based upon the only eyewitness accounts we have."

"Eyewitness accounts?" he asked. Like many people, he'd never considered the Scriptures that way. As a matter of fact, he knew almost nothing about the Bible.

"Sure. The Gospels were written by people who knew Jesus and bore witness to everything He said and did."

Years ago, a few Washington friends in what is informally known as "The Fellowship" had assembled an ingenious compilation of the Gospels. They recognized that newcomers to the

Scriptures are confused by the presence of four biographies of Jesus, one after the other. Each one has a slightly different perspective and different emphases, but where to begin? The group of friends took all the accounts and placed them in the best chronological order, using the most descriptive account of each miracle or teaching.

The group also took out the chapters and verses—which, of course, were added centuries later—as well as notes or commentary of any kind. The result was a no-hassle composite gospel—the ideal life story of Jesus for modern readers. They called it *The Life of Jesus*. A simplified title for a straightforward, simplified account.

When I looked at their slim volume, I was amazed that all our eyewitness accounts of Jesus can be read in two or three hours. The compilers wanted people of all faiths (or no faith) to be able to learn about Jesus from the highest authority and with the fewest obstacles.

I happily gave my friend a copy and asked him to read the little book and report back. He called me a few days later to let me know he just loved the book. It's hard for many of us to imagine, but here was someone who had never known anything at all about Jesus. Every act and every word of teaching was fascinating to him. He'd taken to carrying the book with him wherever he went. I chuckled when I realized I hadn't given him any other information about what he was reading. I hadn't wanted to bias him or burden him with surplus information—that was the whole purpose of the little volume. But now it was time to provide him with some background.

"You're reading what we call the Gospels," I explained. "Every word of them has been taken from Scripture, from four accounts known as Matthew, Mark, Luke, and John—the books are named after their writers—as well as the first chapter of the book of Acts, which Luke also wrote. All of this was written down a few years after Jesus' life on earth."

My friend listened with deep interest and I knew, once again, that there's something about the name of Jesus. People from every culture respond to his life and words, two thousand years after the fact. We take it all for granted in our country, but when Jesus is new to someone, He gets a reaction. In other cultures, where there is none of our cultural baggage, it's usually a positive one.

My friend told me that he was praying to Jesus every day, and as a result, he wondered if there might be some Christian *prayers* I could loan him.

I thought a second, then smiled and told him, "Well, you've actually read the best one of all. Do you remember when the disciples asked Jesus to teach them to pray? It begins, 'Our Father.' We call it the Lord's Prayer."

My friend was quickly on it, finding that prayer and making it his own.

Then, fairly recently, I received an anxious voicemail. My friend had an important question about God, he said, and he wanted to meet right away to talk about it. I called him immediately and asked him to breakfast the following morning.

When we were together, he said, "I now know that the greatest of all the commandments is to love God with all my heart, all my soul, and all my mind. This is interesting! But my question is, how do I do that?"

My mind went totally blank. Such a simple question. So, why was my mind blank? I realized he had asked me what is perhaps the most important of all questions, and I didn't know what to say. I told him I'd need to give this one some thought and more than a little prayer.

I left and pondered this question at great length. How do I actively and truly love God? We think of love as a feeling, but I know that in this case it's more than that. I have to *do* something. But what? How do I show God that I indeed love Him? I couldn't come up with an answer that seemed like the right one to give my friend.

I called one of the compilers of *The Life of Jesus*, my friend and mentor in Washington, DC. I told him his little edition of the Gospels had been taken to heart and inspired a very good question, and I asked for his help with the answer.

He paused briefly, then gave me the best advice for any question related to the study of Scripture. He told me to go back to the source, look at the context, and try to think about what Jesus was trying to say at that moment. Too often we extract individual verses and puzzle over them in a vacuum, when the clues to their meaning are right there in the story. "Turn there right now," he said. "You'll find it in Matthew 22."

As he waited over the telephone line, I flipped to that chapter and read the following:

> Jesus replied: "'Love the Lord your God with all your heart and with all your soul and with all your mind.' This is the first and greatest commandment. And the second is like it: 'Love your neighbor as yourself.' All the Law and the Prophets hang on these two commandments." (Matthew 22:37–40)

When I finished reading, my friend said, quite simply, "There you go."

And I saw it. For the first time, I saw the strategy Jesus was laying out for loving God. He gave the greatest commandment—one my Hindu friend had focused on—but immediately offered the second that was "like it." Clearly the two are tied in together, and Jesus also said that all the Scriptures hang on these two commandments.

That's quite a statement, and it seems evident to me that you have to take these two commandments together.

While some would answer my Hindu friend's question in terms of prayer and worship, here is the best answer I can produce: while those are good ways to show my love to God, the best demonstration of that love comes when I love my neighbor. Of course, that simply raises another question, and according to Luke 10:25, an "expert in the law" asked it immediately. The way he put it was, "Who is my neighbor?" (v. 29).

Jesus gave His answer by describing the actions of the Good Samaritan—someone who came to the aid of a man who was not only in distress but who was also someone others would ignore. This tells me that loving God means loving my neighbor which, in turn, means offering a hand to those who need it deeply—no matter who they are.

It means positioning myself as a "weight-bearing" member of the human race. It means loving and forgiving my enemies—practicing the precept of doing for others the very things I'd want done for myself. Luke 10 brings it all together—we best love God by loving our neighbor, and we're told exactly who that neighbor is: the one in distress.

All of this is so simple, yet seemingly so difficult for me to do. I came to a new realization that it was the only practical way to demonstrate my love for God. Not that this makes the goal any easier for me, particularly when I find myself caught up in the mess of everyday life.

There was a day like that when nothing was going my way. It was one of those days you file under "sheer frustration" and try to forget later. My friend from Ethiopia, Tekle Selassie, describes that experience as being "in the cyclotron" (a type of particle accelerator), and I definitely found the particles of my life accelerating that day. I'd been behind schedule since morning, and now I was dashing from my office to a late afternoon meeting—and I just happened to be jaywalking across Second Avenue and trying to ignore the angry horns and gestures from drivers.

I made it safely to the opposite sidewalk, where I immediately ran into a young couple pushing a baby stroller. These parents had anxious looks on their faces. The man looked directly into my eyes and said, "Mister, we're having a time of great trouble right now. I'm wondering if you might be willing to help us?"

I looked at his wife, who was bent over the carriage, tending to a baby wrapped in a blanket. The child's huge brown eyes peered out at me. Then I looked back at the father and found I couldn't hold the intensity of that gaze. I quickly reached into my wallet and pulled out a fifty-dollar bill, slapping it into his hand. "Here you go," I said, and resumed my dash to the meeting.

Over my shoulder, I heard a faint reply, "Thank you, kind sir. May God bless you." But within minutes I was inside my building, almost to the meeting—and I stopped dead in my tracks.

What was it about the moment that I couldn't hold the young man's gaze? Was I in so much of a hurry that I couldn't look a hurting soul in the eye? Why hadn't I so much as asked what the couple's "great trouble" was? I'd shown no interest, simply throwing money at the problem and hurrying away. I was overcome with a powerful sense of guilt, and I pulled an about-face and headed back out to the sidewalk.

The couple was no longer there. I stepped out to the street and looked as far as I could in both directions. Gone. I ran down to the first intersection on my left and checked down it. Nothing. I actually sprinted up the street to the intersection that lay in the other direction. No chance. It was as if the little family had never been there in the first place.

This isn't about showing what a nice person I am. Professional panhandling is a problem in Minneapolis, and while I try my best to be discerning of real need, I hate to admit I have occasionally walked on the other side of the street to avoid solicitors.

But this was different. I knew that on this day, I was supposed to do something for the young family in my path. I had an overwhelming feeling of sadness. I'd failed a critical test.

Sometimes we walk over to the other side of the street because we don't want to get involved—we're afraid. Why did the "chicken" cross the road? The answer is in that story of the Good Samaritan.

I thought about another cautionary parable from Jesus, when He was talking about separating the sheep from the goats in Matthew 25. The "goats" were those who didn't bring Him a cup of water when He was thirsty or clothe Him when He was naked.

The goats wanted to know exactly when they hadn't given Him water or clothing, and He answered, "Truly I tell you, whatever you did not do for one of the least of these, you did not do for me" (Matthew 25:45).

For years, I missed the significance of the word *one*. That word changes everything. It makes my assignment personal rather than theoretical. That young man with the hurting eyes, the one who asked me for help—he was my one. That baby might as well have been the Christ child, according to Jesus, and the parents Joseph and Mary. I had walked away—no room in the agenda—and I had done it unto Jesus. I was a goat.

I've always thought of myself as a Good Samaritan of sorts. I love helping others, and on most occasions will go out of my way to do so. But this experience, particularly taken with my understanding of how we love God, changed my perspective. Was I a Good Samaritan of convenience? How many of my "ones" had I stepped over, walked around, looked past, and failed to engage?

In particular, my vision was to help the poor on a wider scale. I liked helping masses of people. But Jesus said the test came in ones. He made people as individuals, not demographics. He wants us to minister to them up close and personal.

Cris Carter is an NFL Hall of Famer, a wide receiver for our Minnesota Vikings. Cris attended one of our Tuesday prayer groups, having played a *Monday Night Football* game just the previous evening—and we were meeting at 6:45 a.m., miles across town, in a little coffee shop.

His attendance changed the dynamics of our little meeting,

of course. He was quickly surrounded by many patrons, most of them thrusting pieces of paper or coffee cups in his direction for an autograph. Cameras were snapping pictures. Even the owner wanted a photo from behind the counter, and Cris smiled and agreed.

Once we were gathered around the table, we all thanked Cris for the effort he'd made in joining us no more than seven or eight hours after an intensely physical, hard-fought professional football game.

"Oh, it's not a big deal at all," Cris said, and it was clear he meant it. He went on to tell us during the meeting, "I begin my day the same way every day at 5:30 a.m. I start with a prayer: 'Lord, please put at least one person in my path today, for whom I can reflect your grace, love, and joy.'"

With more than a little trepidation, I did my usual thing and threw out the question that was on my mind. "I really have a hard time believing that's true," I said. "Just a few minutes ago, as early as a quarter to seven, you were surrounded by adoring fans, each of whom wanted a piece of you. Can you really be asking God to put people into your life?"

"That's why I do it," said Cris, looking toward the counter where the commotion had been. "Because once I've said that prayer, any of those people might be the one."

18

Go and Do Likewise

Finding My Purpose and the Ride of My Life

Actions speak louder than words
but not nearly as often.

—MARK TWAIN

The two most important days in your life are the day you are
born and the day you find out why.

—MARK TWAIN

I had given up reading books about Christianity.
I'd been working all these things out: How do I love God? What does Jesus want me to do for people in need? What is the role of faith and the church in actually living out what God wants me to do?

Like anybody else, I tried reading up. There's no shortage of Christian books, in case you haven't noticed. "Of making many books there is no end, and much study wearies the body" (Ecclesiastes 12:12). Translation: the books never stop coming, and trying to read them all wears you out. It's true. I found myself pulled this way and that by various theological perspectives. Who has it right? Your guess is as good as mine.

Finally, I decided to try figuring things out on my own through prayer and reading Scripture. Jesus without the filter.

When a close friend of mine handed me a copy of Rick

Warren's *The Purpose Driven Life*, I smiled, thanked him for the gift, then put the volume aside as soon as I got home.

A few months later, the book found its way back to me in the hands of my wife. She brought it to me and asked, "Have you read this?"

"No," I replied. "In fact, I thought I threw it away."

"You did. But I saved it, and I'm thinking this is one book you might like."

No thanks, I thought, and went back to what I was doing.

But that night, when I went to bed, the covers were pulled down, the reading lamp was on, and there against the pillow was *The Purpose Driven Life*.

I gave up and decided I might as well take a peek. I knew, of course, that this wasn't just another book. Warren's book was a phenomenon, selling more copies than any other nonfiction book other than the Bible. Remarkable, so many people flocking to buy a book promising to help them discover a purpose in life. That told me a lot about the world today.

I opened to the first page and was floored. The very first sentence read, "It's not about you." Readers always seem to notice that famous opening sentence. It goes against the grain of everything we know about people who buy self-help books. Most of the time they're hoping the book is *all* about them. "It's not about you" isn't a winning line to drop into a conversation.

But Rick Warren understands that self-absorption is the worst way to find a purpose in life. I'd found mine by this time. When I climbed into bed and opened to the first page, I was dedicated to helping the poor in Africa. I fully understood that it wasn't all about me—that was the whole point.

That's why I had a difficult time when people complimented me or spoke in glowing terms about my willingness to help others in need. Something felt wrong in those moments, and it took me years to figure out just what.

Up until 1993, when my trip to Africa turned my view of life inside out during my fortieth year, it was all about me. I spent my entire business career racing to get ahead. I know that I should love God, family, and career in that order. But during my earlier career, I generally had things in reverse order. My use of time, energy, and thought would have borne that out.

What Africa did was show me a purpose bigger than myself, something that made my former career goals look pale and insignificant. In Stephen Covey's phrase, I realized that my ladder of success was leaning against the wrong wall. What a wonderful relief it was to let it finally stop being all about me. For the first time, I connected purpose to service.

As I launched into the work of caring for others, I realized that other people saw me making "sacrifices." Now, "do-goodism," as people think of it, seems as dull as it is earnest. In the eyes of these friends and acquaintances, I was "giving up" things—time and money, for example—to serve people across the world. Having wealth offered the possibility to have what they considered fun, and in their eyes I was forgoing that fun.

But for me it didn't feel like sacrifice at all. This *was* my fun. That's what made it my purpose. Since I was made to do it, I was made to enjoy it. Service was joy and adventure. For the first time, I had a calling, and it was so much more exciting than wealth accumulation and traditional ladder climbing.

Before 1993, I'd had the same misperceptions as my friends and acquaintances. Service to others (and especially to the poor) was noble and boring. I'd seen the missionary slide shows. I'd listened to fund-raising pitches about this need or that disaster. I admired the do-gooders but felt no attraction to their pursuit; in fact, I found it boring.

Then I stood on African soil, experienced a kaleidoscope of events and experiences, and all those perceptions changed. My heart opened to a new system of values. It was a gift, as I see it now—perhaps the greatest gift of my life. The notion that we can, in some very small way, serve the "least of these" in the name of Jesus is astonishing and thrilling to me.

Here's something else I've figured out. My calling and yours will differ. God called me to Africa and to the poor, but He obviously calls others to different needs.

I wonder how many people never do find their purpose. The still, soft voice of God is often drowned out by the noise of the world. Even though I've found my calling, it's still a constant struggle to hear God's voice. Ridiculous schedules of mostly irrelevant matters can deafen my ears. The urgent trumps the important, the secular trumps the sacred. But God's will is always there for me to find. The big question is whether I really want to find it.

Like most people, I can be comfortable at church hearing about what Jesus told me to do. But I may grow uncomfortable when pressed to put those words into action. Even now, even with my purpose settled, the hypocrite lives on within me.

Recently, I heard about the world's shortest sermon—an idea that sounds pretty good at first. The pastor stands before his congregation and announces that his sermon will have three parts. "Part one," he says, "is that there are two billion people in the world who are starving to death as we speak. Part two is that most of you don't give a damn about that. Part three is that most of you are more concerned that I said *damn* in church than that two billion people are starving."

It may be more than the world's shortest sermon—it may also be the most revealing. And hearing about it brought me once again to that parable of the Good Samaritan.

Jesus told about the one man who was willing to rescue a wounded soul; how he picked him up, bandaged his wounds, and took him to an inn, making a commitment to remain responsible for the patient. This, Jesus pointed out, was what a neighbor does.

Then He closed out the moment with these words: "Go and do likewise" (Luke 10:37).

That's the calling I hear, the marching orders for my purpose-filled life. I was created by God with various gifts and skills, all of them intended to be used for fulfilling the assignment God gave me. First, I had to wrap my head around the fact that God actually created me with a purpose in mind. (How cool is that?) From there, it became the adventure of a lifetime to figure out what that calling was and how to do it.

Jesus left out one thing when He told that story. Maybe it was meant to be a surprise. The part He didn't mention was that "doing likewise" is no dull obligation at all; rather, it's a life filled with deep joy and true significance. It's living a life that matters.

19

Far from Boring

Not Just Potluck Casseroles
in Church Basements ...
and My Fifteen Minutes of Fame

It is one of the most beautiful compensations of life,
that no man can sincerely try to help another
without helping himself.

— RALPH WALDO EMERSON

Selfishness is when we pursue gain at the expense of others.
But God doesn't have a limited number of treasures to
distribute. When you store up treasures for yourself in heaven,
it doesn't reduce the treasures available to others. In fact, it is
by serving God and others that we store up heavenly treasures.
Everyone gains; no one loses.

—RANDY ALCORN

I came to my own understanding of what it means to serve God.
I built my personal philosophy of life around the story of the
Good Samaritan, the idea that every hurting person is my neigh-
bor, and that I'm to "go and do likewise."

I set about to follow that calling along the path that seemed
clear to me: bringing attention to the problems of Africa, and
doing what little I could to serve there. As I've also said, this never
felt like an obligation of any type—it was pure joy and a sense of
fulfillment I'd never experienced.

As a decade flew by after God got my attention on that first trip overseas, I encountered what are known as unintended consequences. Part of that, of course, is that when we set out to serve someone else, we tend to be the ones who receive the greatest blessing. That's obvious enough. But we also attract a certain amount of attention, which—if we're doing these things for the right reasons—we may not exactly welcome. For various reasons, people shine the spotlight, and suddenly there are new obligations that weren't part of your original plan.

Let me explain what I mean.

On a busy day in 2004, my assistant told me the White House was on line two—over the intercom, no less. Immediately I smelled a prank, and I certainly had the rogue's gallery of friends capable of such an exploit. I picked up the phone, listened to the president's spokesman identify himself, then heard, "Good afternoon, Mr. Brehm. I'm pleased to inform you that President Bush would like to nominate you as chairman of the United States African Development Foundation."

It was clearly legit, so I was stunned. Somehow I managed to state that it would be my honor to serve our president, this nation, and the continent of Africa.

USADF is a small and relatively obscure governmental agency, but I did know a bit about it. Senator Jim Inhofe of Oklahoma had run into a group of Americans beside a pool in Benin, West Africa. "What are you guys doing here in Benin?" he asked with curiosity.

"We are giving away American taxpayers' money," chuckled one of them.

"Really?" said the senator. "So how do you come to be sitting around a pool having a beer?"

"What business is that of yours?"

"I'm a US senator," he replied.

The men, now pale-faced, said nothing.

Senator Inhofe was just beginning his own enduring love affair with the African people. In the Senate, he's now the recognized authority and advocate when it comes to that subject. What's more, he has befriended countless heads of state and government leaders, based on the principles and precepts of Jesus.

He flew home from Benin and made inquiries about USADF—the agency sponsoring the pool group. He discovered that back in 1980, Senator Ted Kennedy had initiated the effort to help Africans help themselves out of poverty at the grassroots level, using principles of entrepreneurship and enterprise.

That actually sounded like a pretty good idea. But you know how it goes—good intentions pave the road to useless bureaucracy. Eventually, USADF had begun morphing in the direction of another top-down government African handout program.

Now it was my turn to be part of all this, and I had little patience with "government as usual," the throwing of money at needs without even taking good aim. I wasn't certain what to expect from my first board meeting. The law provided for seven board members, five from the private sector and two from the US federal government. We had only two others: Jack Leslie, from the public relations world, and Dr. Ephraim W. Batambuze, a cardiologist born in Uganda.

I was out of my depth during the first year. I didn't even speak the language of bureaucracy and was asked to sign off on things I wasn't totally clear about. What did "community development" involve? What was "capacity building" exactly? It was overwhelming.

There were also political questions. I was what I'd now term a "moderate conservative," and across the table was Jack Leslie, whom I knew to be a New York liberal. I was braced for the conflict certain to come—but it never came. Instead, I realized after some time that we'd become very close friends. More than a decade later, including several years with Jack as the chairman, we have yet to encounter a disagreement. If such nonpartisan relationships were possible, then what did that say for our potential as a group? We could become a leading edge in providing enterprise-driven ideas and innovations.

There had been a vision for fighting poverty through enterprise, but what had been lost was the basic principle of working with the poor on a grassroots level. Jack and I, bonded in our desire to get back to those basics, worked through a brutal and highly stressful reorganization. We succeeded in forming a strong bipartisan alliance of political advocates on Capitol Hill, and we even doubled our tiny budget.

Not that any of this helped my popularity among staff. I appeared to some as a rightwing capitalist zealot, intent on remaking USADF in my conservative image. Sensing the incredulity among some of the other board members, I called a staff meeting and made two statements.

First, I'd go toe-to-toe with anyone in the room *or* in Africa regarding my compassion for that continent's poor. And it was worth mentioning that other than Jack and Ephraim, I was the only one in the room not receiving a paycheck.

Second, I challenged the group to take me to a single village in Africa where the tactics of "community development, capacity building, and sustainability" had helped poverty in the least. If they could find that village, I'd eat my hat.

Response: silence.

The USADF was twenty-five years old, and no such example could be found. And it's often observed that the definition of insanity is doing the same thing over and over again, and expecting different results, so Jack and I were determined to change course.

An example of the old way came on my first trip to Africa on an official basis. In Kampala, Uganda, I received an invitation from the embassy to come to a reception. The purpose was to introduce USADF to the donor community. I wasn't sure what that meant, but upon entering the elegant embassy boardroom, I saw about thirty people who represented various government and nongovernment agencies in Uganda.

As the meeting moved on, the chargé d'affaires noticed how quiet I'd been. He wanted to know if I had any comments or questions.

I replied that I had two. First, having listened intently and done my very best, I had to admit I had no idea what anyone was talking about. It was in a language I had not yet learned—even though it was an English-speaking room. Sometimes I felt like I was getting it, but then, two or three acronyms linked together lost me again.

Everybody laughed and apologized for what I refer to as "development speak." I then offered my second observation. In thirty minutes, I'd heard references to conferences and meetings in Europe, Washington, and other places. What I hadn't heard was a single mention of the poor.

Apparently, my own language was clear. It was met by silence.

All of these people, I'm sure, had the best of intentions. But it's so easy to get caught up in the machinery of bureaucracy and lose the mission of helping the poor not be poor anymore. That goal is so simple, so elegant. And we cover it up with strategies and agendas and details until the goal vanishes and is lost.

Thankfully, in time, we at USADF raised awareness of what we were about by achieving practical results. We did in fact reduce poverty with the creation of co-ops and small and medium-size enterprises. We tried to keep it simple and practical and eliminate the extraneous. The image we used for ourselves was that of a speedboat in a bay of ocean liners. We're now seen as pioneers in creative solutions for helping the poor help themselves in Africa. And now, we're seeing private equity firms lining up to make direct investments into a fast-growing sector, creating jobs and capital within a past culture of hopeless poverty.

A few years into this experience, another phone call changed my life. The moment is etched in my memory: it was 5:30 p.m. on Friday, January 11, 2008. I was sitting down to watch the nightly news in Minneapolis when the phone rang. It was Senator Michael Enzi from Wyoming.

Mike and I had friendship that sprang from our common love for the people of Africa. But why would he be calling around dinnertime on a Friday evening?

Mike asked me to speak at the National Prayer Breakfast in Washington the following month. Once again, I knew this wasn't a prank—not from Mike.

I knew that the breakfast had been an annual tradition since President Eisenhower started it with a few friends. It had grown to become a rather momentous event attended by the president and the First Lady, cabinet members, congressional leaders, and other leaders from across the world—about four thousand people from every race, creed, culture, and nation. Mother Teresa, Bono, and Tony Blair have been among recent speakers. The gathering is based on the principles of Jesus and nothing else.

I didn't know how to respond to Mike's invitation over the phone. I mean that literally—he asked if I was still on the line after a few seconds of silence. The only response that came to mind for me was, "You've got to be kidding."

"No, Ward, I'm not," he chuckled. "We want you to be the speaker."

I told him I'd need to do some thinking and praying—after I stopped my head from spinning. That's what he'd expected, of course, and he asked if I could let him know something within a few days. Also, he'd pray for me.

"Are you all right?" asked Kris when she saw my demeanor as I returned to the family room.

"I'm not sure," I said. I told her about the call, and, echoing my response, she said, "You've got to be kidding." We took a few minutes to pray together for guidance.

That sounds pious, but let me add some honesty. Over the next few days, as I thought of the event, I muttered under my breath, "Are you kidding me?" It was overwhelming. I felt that I was in way over my head.

On Sunday, my son Andy asked, "Dad, are you okay?"

"Sure," I said. "Why?"

"Because all day today you've been walking around the house, quietly saying, 'Are you kidding me?'"

My utterances hadn't been as "under my breath" as I thought they were.

By that evening, I realized I had no choice. I couldn't turn down a request that was caught up with my sense of calling. Plus, I'd very literally felt a calling to do this, and it was a genuinely stunning opportunity. But what would I say? And what if I flopped, as seemed likely?

I believe that with my feelings of inadequacy, God had me exactly where He wanted me, because I had no options other than to call on Him for help.

Thus began what I call my "Moses period," in that I was as solemn and stoic as the old patriarch with his long beard and a pair of tablets under his arm. This seemed appropriate until Kris suggested that just maybe I should look upon this breakfast as something fun.

I stopped in my tracks and realized she had a point. This thing was very, very cool. I would be meeting the president. He would be listening to me speak. And I would look out across an audience that represented leaders from all over the world.

Something amazing happened as we boarded the plane to the nation's capital. I realized I wasn't even nervous. I had my speech written down, and I felt good about it. My whole family was with me, including my mom and my brother Steve. Only my daughter, Sarah, who was studying abroad in Australia, couldn't make it. I went to bed that night, slept like a baby, and felt good the next morning.

I was actually able to enjoy the privilege of sitting at the head table with George and Laura Bush. There was prayer, singing, and the reading of Scripture. Then Mike Enzi introduced me to the audience.

Looking back, I wish I could recall it with the precision of high-definition video. I can't, but I do recall being calm, collected, and able to speak with authority. I wasn't foolish enough to believe it had anything to do with me, however. I knew God was with me, and as He always does, He offered His power to do His work. I described the sensation later as being like a trumpet through which God played His song.

The message was well received in spite of my being a nobody— as a matter of fact, *because* of my being a nobody, as I came to believe. Traditionally the speaker isn't announced until the morning of the Breakfast, but usually it's someone well-known.

Not me. Friends of mine scattered through the ballroom heard a buzz through the crowd. "Who is this guy?" The phrase echoed around the huge ballroom.

"Anybody heard of him?"

The answer was largely a disappointed, "Nope."

The reality is that a person's message is often filtered through his reputation. When a movie star or sports personality speaks, we hear it in context of what we know about them. But I spoke from a kind of reputational vacuum. People were forced to listen to my message with fresh ears because I had no social standing to get in the way.

My fifteen minutes of fame were over quickly, which was fine with me. All these things were part of the unintended consequences of my path, and as such, not so bad. It was a humbling yet thrilling experience that will stay with me for the rest of my life. This notion of trying to follow Jesus has been the epitome of exploration and adventure that for me has made all of my secular pursuits tame by comparison.

20

Two Presidents and a Few More Minutes of Fame

Humbled by Moments of Privilege

> Humility is like underwear;
> essential, but indecent if it shows.
> —Helen Nielsen

> Don't be so humble, you're not that great.
> —Golda Meir

I had to conclude that I'd found myself moving in directions and going places I'd never have imagined. I had to consider my horizons broadened.

Yet I still had one of those "Is this really happening?" moments when, in 2008, I was again told that the White House was calling. I suppose one never becomes accustomed to those words.

When I picked up the phone, a rather formal voice informed me that President Bush had decided to award me with a medal. I must have replied with some degree of incredulity, because he then repeated himself and specified that it was the Presidential Citizens Medal I was to receive. Further, he stated, it was second only to the Presidential Medal of Freedom.

Of course, for me, there had been honor enough in being

asked to serve the poor through USADF. That was incredibly humbling. That was something I could see as giving. This felt a little like receiving. Did I really need a medal?

I replied that I wasn't too sure about this.

"May I ask why, Mr. Brehm?"

"Well," I said, with a deep breath, "it has something to do with my faith. You see, as a follower of Jesus, I'm taught that if we receive our reward here on earth, then that's our reward—instead of receiving one in heaven."

I wondered what he must think of me as there was a pause on the other end of the line. Then, in his formal and proper style, he said, "Well, sir, technically, this is not a 'reward'—it's a medal."

Kris and I ignored my no-doubt superficial humility issues and flew to Washington with our family for an Oval Office ceremony. Once I'd accepted the idea of doing it, of course, I realized just what a unique, memorable, and downright cool experience it is to make a trip there—one of the most rewarding experiences of my life, even if it was a medal.

We gathered in a small room in the West Wing of the White House. There were a number of other recipients, many of whom I couldn't identify. I did recognize Gary Sinise, the actor, and Chuck Colson, the Watergate personality and later founder of Prison Fellowship—both with their own families. We waited with eagerness and more than a little nervousness.

One of the president's assistants walked in quietly and asked us to follow her out into a hallway.

I thought about my earlier connection to this office. My oldest son, Andy, worked in the West Wing as an intern for Ari Fleischer, press secretary under President Bush. On his first day of work, Andy was as awestruck as I was now.

Now, as we waited in the hallway, Andy said, "Dad, see that door? It goes directly into the Oval Office." It was three feet away.

After a few minutes, it swung open and there stood a beaming

George W. Bush. "Hey, dude," he said. "What are you doing standing around out there? Come on in." Really, those were his exact words.

It was a surreal moment, one that words can't adequately paint—standing at the epicenter of world power and influence, in an office as familiar to me from the news and other imagery as my own home. My family chatting with President and First Lady Bush.

If anyone from our group was calm and collected, it was my eighty-four-year-old mother. The most awed was my son Mike, who is usually socially comfortable and outgoing. He was speechless now.

I'd met the First Lady on several other occasions, so we talked comfortably now. Then the president and I talked a bit about Africa as well as the current economic crisis, which weighed heavily on everyone's mind that year.

Every aspect of the experience was amazing. We were never hurried along, but eventually the time came for the presentation of the medals by the president, in front of his desk. He placed the medals around my neck and shook my hand. My family stepped in for a group picture.

We were then escorted down the hallway to the State Dining Room, where members of the Marine Chamber Orchestra were playing lovely classical music. I literally bumped into Chuck Colson, whom I'd also met a few years earlier in Minnesota.

In the state I was in, I could do little more than babble about the feeling of being there at the White House and meeting a president. Then, catching myself, I said, "Of course, you worked here for years, Chuck. And you've come back on many occasions, I'm sure. I guess there wouldn't be the same impact for you."

He gave me a rather grave look. "Ward, if any person enters the Oval Office, for any reason, and they don't feel a sense of overwhelming awe and deep humility—they don't belong there."

President Eisenhower called it the loneliest place in the world. Now I understood what he meant. You enter by narrowing concentric circles: the White House, then the West Wing, and finally the Oval Office itself. And your sense of awe and wonder increases the closer your approach to that nucleus. There's actually a genuine touch of fear. And you come away with a far stronger impression of the need to pray for the man who occupies that lonely place—even if you don't agree with his policies. How foolish are we not to pray for the man who guides our country? We can always pray for his wisdom, his discernment, and his humility.

That was a great day, but there were others too. My new position with the USADF brought a number of opportunities that I consistently found exciting. For example, in 2006, the Bushes asked Kris and me to attend a state luncheon in honor of the newly elected president of Liberia, Ellen Johnson Sirleaf.

I knew that Liberia was emerging from a civil war filled with bloodshed and terror under the despot Charles Taylor. News accounts had been horror stories revolving around child soldiers and young girls serving as "wives" to marauding bands of military soldiers. But now, hope was emerging under a new leader, the product of a democratic election.

We flew to Washington and arrived at the east gate right on time. President Bush and the First Lady greeted us, along with President Johnson Sirleaf, and we exchanged pleasantries and briefly discussed USADF. Then we were escorted to the magnificent State Dining Room—though, believe me, as you walk through the White House, every hallway makes you want to stop, take a closer look, and ask questions about the history of that location. You simply never get used to being in a place like that.

At the luncheon, couples were intentionally seated at separate tables. I met some new friends at my table, including National Security Advisor Stephen Hadley, who had recently replaced Condoleezza Rice. Between us was Madison Tukpah, the national security advisor for Liberia. And I quickly recognized Karen Hughes, the president's chief advisor, across the table. Scanning the room, I recognized names and faces I knew only from the nightly news.

As a world-renowned string quartet played for us, a very fine lunch was served. Madison Tukpah politely asked how I'd been invited to the luncheon, and I told him about USADF. That got his interest immediately, and he followed up with questions of all kinds. For him, the intriguing point was that a very small government agency was the only arm of the US government capable of making direct investments into African enterprises.

I did my best to give him an overview of our strategy and how we worked. We could make grants up to $250,000 into small- and medium-size businesses, with the goal of creating employment and direct trade opportunities.

Again, Tukpah seemed captivated by our subject. "Would you please remain here at the table after the luncheon is concluded?" he asked. "I wish to introduce you to a friend from Monrovia, so that we can speak in more detail."

"It would be my honor." I smiled.

The moment the luncheon activities came to a conclusion, my friend left and returned with Steven Tolbert, an investment banker from New York who had recently returned to Monrovia (the capital city of Liberia) to serve President Johnson Sirleaf as a trade representative. He, too, was excited by my description of what USADF was doing. I tried to gently make the point that we were only a tiny agency capable of making relatively small grants.

To these two, that wasn't the point. Tolbert wanted to know if I might be willing to meet with President Johnson Sirleaf that very evening to discuss the possibility of opening a program in Liberia. I was exhilarated by some of the discussions I was now having because of this luncheon—which, in itself, had been such a special occasion in my life.

Later that day, President Johnson Sirleaf made both a plea and an invitation. She indicated she would be making a speech tomorrow to the joint sessions of Congress. She was already aware of large financial pledges, for relief and development, that the US government would be making for Liberia. The problem was that for her country to receive this aid, months would need to pass. And when she returned, her people, having been traumatized by the recent war, as well as being deeply impoverished, would be expecting more immediate change. She asked if there was any way USADF could come open a program now.

After I discussed this quickly with USADF Vice-Chairman Jack Leslie and President Rod MacAlister, we immediately said yes. Within ten days, we found ourselves in Monrovia. Glancing at the newspaper on our first morning, I saw that USADF had made headlines. Even as it seemed important to manage expectations, at every turn we encountered excitement and eagerness for any level of help we could facilitate. We were scheduled to meet with President Johnson Sirleaf the following day.

When we met to sign the country accords and various agreements, we mentioned one more time the relatively small amount of our commitment. The president beamed back at us, her eyes brilliant, and said, "Yes, but this is real! *This* is the type of direct investment Liberia needs most. As I return to Liberia, I'm expected to bring back some report, some tangible hope for the people. You have given me precisely that, and we will always be grateful to USADF."

My term as chairman of the agency came to a close, and President Obama appointed Jack Leslie to take my place, while also reappointing me to the board. I couldn't have been more encouraged. Jack brought a new and much needed vision for helping the most marginalized people on the planet, those living in conflict zones. Because USADF employs only Africans, we can operate where American personnel cannot. To those living in active conflict zones, as well as others far off the grid, Jack brought the promise of income generation through small enterprise and career training.

We now operate in Somalia, Mali, Niger, and other places where others fear to tread. It's been said that when the roads end, USADF's mission begins.

As I think back to the beginning of my change in life direction—my very personal desire to serve Africa in some way—I'm met with a question: who'd have thought I'd meet in the Oval Office and across the world with presidents? God's plans and timing are often unfathomable to us, and sometimes I think He reveals them one small step at a time so we won't see what's coming and chicken out.

21

Speak of the Devil

Coming to Grips with the Reality of Evil

✦━✦━✦

Don't ever try to argue with the Devil.
—Rick Warren

The devil's greatest disguise in the Western World
had been to convince us that he doesn't exist.
—Dr. Mark Jacobsen

Most people imagine the devil as a cartoon character in a red
suit with a forked tail. Not me. I've seen too much of his
work, and there's nothing cute or cartoonish about any of it. I've
had heartrending experiences in the presence of pure evil and its
aftermath.

In my quest to repay Africa for the significance it's provided
my life, I've had both the blessing of seeing God's presence and
the triumph of good as well as witnessing the unimaginable heartbreak of unspeakable evil. It seems to me that if I believe in the
reality of a loving and personal God, I must also accept the literal
existence of aggressive evil and its ageless advocate, satan.

Following the genocide in Rwanda in 1994, I heard the hor-
rific stories of women and children having limbs cut off, then
being thrown into pit latrines to die slowly. I spoke to people who
saw these things happen, and these are terrible moments I'll never
forget.

The perpetrators were often neighbors and friends from different tribes who, for reasons they could never explain afterward, descended into inhuman savagery. That's the nature of pure evil: it feeds on itself like the flames of a burning house that begins with a spark and becomes a raging inferno. More than eight hundred thousand people died in a ninety-day charnel house of genocide in Rwanda. To begin to understand such a number, consider that there were ten thousand murders *each day* for *three months* as the world watched—and did absolutely nothing. Yet, some would have us believe there is no such thing as evil and that notions of morality are just inventions of culture and religion.

It's as difficult to write about these things as I know it is to read them, but at some point, we must all come to grips with the depths of utter godlessness that exists and thrives in this world. I spoke with some of the survivors of kidnapping by The Lord's Resistance Army in Gulu, northern Uganda, who told us of raids by this terrorist group on villages. These raids had the purpose of kidnapping young boys to use as child soldiers and young girls to become sex slaves.

As part of their indoctrination, the boys were forced to rape their mothers as their families were made to watch. If anyone refused, another child would behead a family member until there was compliance. Sons were forced to kill their mothers with a knife. These children became so traumatized they'd follow any order, however cruel.

We're tempted to use words such as *animalistic*, but animals don't perpetrate acts of conscious, intentional, and heightened cruelty such as these. There really are no words that capture the ultimate obscenity of evil unleashed.

Saddest of all, the aggressors in Uganda were none other than the once young and innocent victims of the same terror. It's a cycle of wickedness that renews itself—perpetual-motion evil. So, if you ask if I believe there is a devil, and if evil is more than an idea, yes, I do.

I've been to eastern Congo, where millions of people have died in an "off the grid" war between warring rebel groups. With a military escort, we visited displacement camps that are—again—unworthy of animals, much less human souls. The only hope we glimpsed in the region came at Heal Africa, which was like a tiny hospital outpost in the depths of hell. We saw twenty girls in a small room, some as young as eight years old. They were victims of rape and mutilation at the hands of roving militias, and now they waited quietly for reconstructive surgery.

I found myself weeping beside a lovely young girl whose small frame barely registered beneath a blanket. From such a tiny body, her eyes seemed large and searching. "Why are you crying?" she asked me, her soft words translated by a nurse.

"I'm so sad and very sorry that this has happened to you." These were the only words I could find.

"Don't cry for me. I'm one of the lucky ones allowed to come here. They say they can make me better. Please pray for my sister instead. She was taken into the woods, and no one has seen her since."

I think of 1 Peter 5:8, which tells us, "Your enemy the devil prowls around like a roaring lion looking for someone to devour." Sometimes he prowls throughout whole nations. He was certainly roaming Burundi in the 1990s. The ethnic violence and mayhem of civil war were finally halted there when Nelson Mandela brought the Tutsis and various Hutu forces together through the Arusha Agreement.

But how long will that country experience peace? As of this writing, there is political discord again in Burundi. Fear spreads like a contagion, and people whisper more than converse, share rumors more than small talk, and the threat of violence looms on every street corner.

In the conflict zones of "failed states," deception and corruption, the signs of deeper evil, can be seen everywhere: the ever-present roadblocks and trucks filled with young military soldiers. Many of us familiar with our friends in these dangerous places pray that God will restrain the lion from breaking free.

Many times, I've seen the light shine most gloriously when the darkness seems to have won dominance. These are the times when God loves to show His sovereignty and power and the goodness and decency of those who work in His name.

Another verse from the Bible, and one I find compelling, is James 4:7: "Resist the devil, and he will flee from you." It's such a simple and straightforward verse in the face of something as overwhelming and incomprehensible as evil. It says, yes, there is a devil, and you need only say no to him. Then the devil will retreat. Yet, I realize he is exceptionally clever—the most brilliant of liars, a master of disguising the truth. He used Scripture to tempt Jesus in the wilderness, and similarly he uses half-truths and familiar assumptions to trip us up. John says that "when he lies, he speaks his native language, for he is a liar and the father of lies" (John 8:44). From this I learn that truth is our best defense against him, but we must know the truth from his counterfeited versions of it.

For each cultural group, satan uses the most effective deception that will most effectively trick them. I've heard people in Africa offer stories, seemingly farfetched, of the devil taking human form. But these stories are persistent enough that they become hard to dismiss. Other quite common accounts involve witch doctors performing satanic rites, with the tangible presence of the evil one.

I talked casually over a roaring campfire in the wilderness of the Serengeti Plain with a close friend, a Harvard-educated doctor who had spent the past forty years in Tanzania caring for the poor. He talked rather matter-of-factly about the devil, describing hair-raising examples of true physical manifestations of the devil in tribal settings. Though he trusted these observations with me, he said he was reluctant to tell most people. They'd think he was crazy or prone to exaggeration.

I suspected he'd already noticed my incredulous facial expression; I wasn't sure what to think. He said, "As someone who has spent most of your life in the United States, of course you'd discredit any visible sign of the devil. Satan has the perfect strategy in the Western world: he has you convinced he doesn't exist! This allows him to roam at will in American society." In far corners of Africa, however, people know better.

I heard a little parable about the devil's training academy for up-and-coming demons. On graduation day, he spoke with three class leaders, questioning them about what they had learned. "Now that the time has come to set you loose on the earth," he said, "what strategy will you choose for leading people away from God?"

The first demon replied, "Sir, I'll tell them there is no God."

The devil scowled. "Terrible idea—it won't work! Not until you can find a way for people to stop seeing the beauty of creation. It's impossible to get past that."

The second demon said, "Sir, I'll tell them there's no judgment."

"I'm afraid that won't do either. What are they teaching in these classrooms these days? God planted a sense of right and wrong in every human. They can feel it in their bones that judgment is inevitable. Next?"

The third demon said, "I'll tell them there's a God and there's a judgment. But I'll also tell them there's plenty of time."

The devil laughed and clapped the clever demon on the back. "Fantastic! You've learned well. That lie is the greatest one I ever came up with!"

He was right. It's an effective lie, particularly in America. We always believe there will be time later, particularly for "philosophical" issues like the question of evil. We go back to chasing the things that seem important but are merely urgent.

For me, the reality of evil is no abstract piece of philosophy. Once you've looked into the innocent eyes of a damaged little girl, it becomes a matter of life and death. Nor is there ever "plenty of time"—not when you visit Burundi, the Democratic Republic of the Congo, northern Uganda and other places of conflict. The air is thick with the tension of instability, violence, and the threat of civil war.

No matter how many trips I make to Africa, it won't change the constant need for darkness to be cast out by light. As I grow older, I realize my life is fleeting and that the opportunities to serve God and combat evil are equally fleeting. Thus, the work in Africa has felt, from its very beginning, like urgent business to me.

The devil is constantly working. His mayhem shows up in countless and often unanticipated ways: genocide, disasters, disease, lies, temptation, rationalization, and greed. The storms and murky shadows of evil will always be with us. Jesus made that clear when He said, "In this world you will have trouble" (John 16:33).

Satan's acts of evil are very real and usually cleverly disguised. My greatest defense is to come to grips with the fact that satan's existence is real. From there, I need to be willing to do whatever God asks of me to push back the borders of evil (even if the results seem very slight). If I'm not willing to confront evil, it flourishes. Indeed, how I respond to evil defines who I am.

Sir Edmund Burke was much more eloquent when he said, "The only thing necessary for the triumph of evil is for good men to do nothing."

The Gospel According to a Knucklehead

Bad Things, Good People, Tough Questions

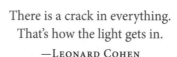

There is a crack in everything.
That's how the light gets in.
—Leonard Cohen

"Sometimes I'd like to ask God why He allows poverty,
suffering, and injustice when He could
do something about it."
"Well, why don't you ask Him?"
"Because I'm afraid He would ask me the same question."
—Anonymous

We've all wondered about it. We've all faced the question on a very personal level. Why do bad things happen to good people? Before I could even attempt to answer that question, I struggled for a long time with the question of what it actually means to believe in God.

A close friend summarized my conclusion better than I ever could: "Science and culture seem to prefer a universe of random happenings. Randomness lets us do whatever we want; it assumes nothing ultimately matters too much anyway. But when we suggest that the universe is governed by choice, we're describing a radically different place. Choice makes all the difference."

I always believed in choice. Before I turned forty, I believed that the point of my life was to choose good actions, to be as good a person as I could, and leave the rest to God. But after years of reading Scripture and being tutored by my heroes in faith—Doug Coe, Arthur Rouner, and Monty Sholund, among many others—I see things very differently.

What follows is my own theology—the gospel according to a knucklehead. It's my attempt to square all that is wrong with a world governed by a good and loving God.

God created the universe and then humanity with a perfect intention. He equipped us with free will so that we, in turn, could choose to return His love voluntarily, as any true relationship dictates.

Sin is humankind's abuse of that free will. The wreckage of the human exercise of free will is all around us today. God never desired or planned for any of it—we've done violence to each other and to God's world through our own stubbornness. Sin reproduces and intertwines itself at every level. It created a full and absolute barrier between a perfect God and us deeply flawed human beings.

So God responded. First, He gave us the instruction manual. Through Moses, He offered the Ten Commandments, and naturally we set about enlarging upon those until we had more than seven hundred "laws" no one could ever hope to learn, much less keep.

Then God did the unthinkable. He bridged the gap between His perfection and our utter failure by taking upon Himself all the sins of those willing to believe in Him. He did this by becoming one of us in the person of Jesus. In one fell swoop, the wall between Creator and creation was forever toppled.

That's why we call eternal life a *gift*. In my own experience, unconditional gifts of great worth are difficult to accept, and this represents the ultimate conceivable gift. Once I have accepted this simple gospel as being true, it's a done deal. All debts are canceled, and that's a promise from God.

We made our choice, God chose to rescue us—and so, where does "being good" fit into this picture? To the extent that I embrace the sacrifice of the cross and the resulting gift, my only appropriate response will come in the form of active gratitude. No longer am I straining to earn God's favor; now I'm freely giving of myself within the joy of a loving friendship. Rather than doing things *for* God, I can make myself available for Him to act *through* me.

This is the simplest possible explanation of an understanding I've spent half a lifetime working out—my take on God, humanity, and the problem between us. But I'm not arrogant enough to suggest I've solved all the great questions of human experience. Like everyone else, I see bad things happen to good people, and I wonder about eternal justice.

Just after His baptism by John, Jesus walked into the desert and spent weeks enduring temptation by the devil. In one of the three temptations, satan showed Jesus all the kingdoms of the earth and said, "All this I will give you ... if you will bow down and worship me" (Matthew 4:9).

Wait a minute. Rewind that tape! That sounds as if the things of earth are the devil's to give. In fact, in another passage Jesus calls him "the prince of this world" (John 16:11). If that's the case, why do we keep asking why bad things happen to good people? It might make more sense to talk about why good things happen to *anybody*. The Scriptures help us understand just how deep the damage is, both within us and around us. How does goodness break through any of that—unless God is at work?

I feel certain God didn't go to the trouble of creating us to be mere robots, programmed in advance to say I love you because we have no other circuitry. What He was after was a true relationship, one that must be chosen. Even Jesus was sent into the wilderness to *choose* God over taking the low road and giving in to satan. And

Jesus simply showed what we could have been like, if we hadn't made the wrong choice.

God's will is perfect; the problem is *me*. With the existence of sin come consequences. Bad things happen. We live in a broken world where people suffer.

I personally don't believe that God controls all circumstances.

Does He control the rape of a young child in eastern Congo? Of course not. Does God will the infant in eastern Congo to die in his mother's arms from starvation? Ridiculous.

Is God's heart broken by the same things that break our hearts? I think so. Did Jesus weep? Yes.

But I also believe that in everything that occurs, God is at work. The famous verse Romans 8:28 gives me that promise. Jesus didn't promise to deliver us from trouble but to be with us in that trouble.

Following the death of his wife, Leslie Weatherhead wrote a book called *The Will of God*. Everything within him rebelled against the notion that God desired his beloved wife to die so young. Weatherhead, giving this much thought, decided that God has, in a sense, *three* wills.

His *original* will intended perfection—a world free of sin or suffering, where we used (but never abused) our free choice.

Through His *circumstantial* will, God works through difficult and tragic circumstances, in ways we may not see, to bring goodness from sorrow.

Finally, there is God's *perfect* will, seen only when all things are put right in heaven, for those who believe.

That understanding resonates with both my experience and what I read in Scripture, with its vast group of characters, even the best of whom suffer deeply. All of them died, many tragically. All of them made poor choices. Nonetheless, Scripture holds them up as heroes. The wisest of the wise, Solomon, spent his final years in perplexity and despair, as related in Ecclesiastes.

The late pastor Vance Havner writes, "God uses broken things. It takes broken soil to produce a crop, broken clouds to give rain, broken grain to give bread, broken bread to give strength. It is the broken alabaster box that gives forth perfume. It is Peter, weeping bitterly, who returns to greater power than ever."[1]

It's been said that suffering either makes you better or makes you bitter. Monty Sholund was fond of saying, "Never miss the privilege of your problem." At first it sounded like total nonsense. But as I pondered the notion I saw a great truth. Often my pain and suffering is the thing that has brought me the most personal growth. Indeed, suffering is a great instructor. In a world that is constantly distracting us with its frenzy of activity, pain and suffering make us stop. They force us to reflect and ponder. They teach us empathy, patience, and humility.

I recall the story of the farmer whose old donkey fell into his dried-up well. He pondered what to do and finally decided the best thing would be to just bury the old donkey by filling the dry well with dirt. He poured shovel after shovel until the hole was nearly full. Later and to his amazement the farmer looked out and saw the old donkey grazing in the field. Only later did he realize that each shovel of dirt he piled on the donkey was shrugged off and after time allowed it to climb out.

When I look back on my own life, I see the truly difficult situations that afforded the most spiritual growth in my life. I was devastated by the loss of my father. Grieving triggered an investigation into questions that led to even greater questions, including that of personal faith. Soon afterward, I came to a personal crossroads on the dusty paths of Africa, where I was finally stripped of all pretenses and, for the first time, understood the calling of Jesus in my life.

Seven years after that, in Africa again, I was challenged to take a solitary walk with a friend I hadn't yet come to trust fully—a trip into the middle of nowhere that made me realize that up to then

I had been a "donor" without really embracing the reality of both the joys and challenges of the community we were trying to help. (I've told that story in my earlier book *White Man Walking*.)

Finally, there was the personal crisis I encountered through my wife's medical diagnosis. Kris' condition was said to be terminal, yet we experienced a miracle. But I know it was the pain more than the victory that taught me the most through that turmoil. And as I write these words, I live with health issues of my own to remind me constantly that we're little more than wisps in the wind. Indeed, "We should never forget the privilege of our problem."

Billy Graham wrote, "Comfort and prosperity have never enriched the world as adversity has done. Out of pain and problems have come the sweetest songs, the most poignant poems, the most gripping stories. Out of suffering and tears have come the greatest spirits and the most blessed lives."[2]

It takes a certain amount of hard-fought wisdom simply to begin accepting that truth. There are priceless lessons God knows we'll learn only through adversity. I understand that better as a father myself. I love my children unconditionally, yet I watch bad things happen in their lives. Rather than rescue them the moment a dark cloud hovers, there are times when I can simply stand with them until the storm passes. It will play a part in their own growth; I accept that, but their pain brings me pain.

God answers every prayer but not always the way we would like Him. Even Jesus was led where He did not want to go. Whenever I get frustrated or angry when that happens, I recall Jesus praying with tears and sweat of blood in the garden of Gethsemane. There He said, "Father, if you are willing, take this cup from me." But then immediately added, "yet not my will, but yours be done" (Luke 22:42). I realize with great chagrin how often I leave out that second part.

I've thought of Jesus, as I imagine many have, as the strong lifeguard who looks out across the beach from His tower. When a young girl is carried out too far and cries out for help, He leaps to the task, knifing through the surf to the side of the drowning girl. But as I've come to understand, perhaps on occasion He can only wrap His arms around the girl and drown with her. It's not the stuff of happy endings, but neither is life as we come to experience it. Tragedy is a given, but feeling the all-encompassing love of God is no small gift in the midst of it.

In *The Purpose Driven Life*, Rick Warren confesses he's keeping a list of all the questions he wants to ask God when he gets to heaven. That's a great idea. There are so many answers I'd love to have, many of them involving questions of suffering: natural tragedies, the death of a child, starving villages.

The world is a great story with many loose ends and unanswered questions, but an ending that is certain: God wins. His perfect will triumphs, and every question will be answered, simply not as quickly as we would choose. Every wrong will be made right. Every tear will be dried. And the ultimate will of God—the one that remains—abides forever.

Kris' Story, Part 1:
In the Eye of the Storm

You Don't Know What You've Got till It's Gone

We are hard pressed on every side, but not crushed;
perplexed, but not in despair; persecuted,
but not abandoned; struck down, but not destroyed.

—2 Corinthians 4:8–9

You never know how much you really believe
anything until its truth or falsehood becomes a matter
of life and death for you. It is easy to say you believe a rope
to be strong and sound as long as you are merely using it
to cord a box. But suppose you had to hang by that
rope over a precipice. Wouldn't you then first discover
how much you really trusted it?

—C. S. Lewis

In March 2009, my wife, Kris, was soaring down the ski slopes at Yellowstone Club. She came home exhausted and exhilarated as usual. But later she came to me with what she said was, "a little problem." Kris was and is slim, but her midsection had swelled up as if she were pregnant.

"How did this happen?" I asked with concern.

She told me she'd felt some changes in that area during the last few months, but she hadn't wanted to get a lot of doctors involved.

Kris is holistic in her approach to health, and she simply didn't believe this was anything to be concerned about.

She was wrong about that. Back in Minneapolis, a CT scan told us we needed to take this thing seriously. There was a large tumor in and around her liver. We needed to get into the Mayo Clinic as soon as possible, and we sought out the best people to help us. The one name we kept coming to was that of Dr. Lewis Roberts, a liver specialist. But quickly we found that Mayo's schedule was full. We could wait a week—except that week might make all the difference.

Kris and I prayed and cried together. Dr. Teferri, my own hematologist and friend, promised to do what he could on our behalf. He actually got us in the next day and arranged that we were to be attended by none other than Dr. Lewis Roberts. We really began to feel maybe there was something more than random chance at work when Dr. Roberts told me he'd read my book *White Man Walking*. He had grown up in Ghana, and during the three-day regimen of Kris' testing, immediately we were bonded through our interest in Africa.

When I asked him where he'd gotten the book, he gave the names of two missionaries, David and Sherry Hall. These were great friends of mine, whom we'd helped to support in ministry for twenty-five years. As we made that connection, he paused a moment before saying, "David and Sherry have been my mentors in following Jesus."

The fingerprints of God were visible and not for the last time.

I always asked every doctor we encountered whether he or she believed in miracles, and, without exception, they said that miracles happened all the time at Mayo.

As the tests came to an end, we gathered for consultation. I felt the shadow of a dark cloud forming above us. Sure enough, the oncologist said Kris had an eight-and-a-half-pound tumor, half inside and half outside her liver. Inoperable. Nothing to be done.

Not even close. Our sympathies. Kris asked how long she had—the answer was a few weeks to a few months.

It was one of those moments when reality seems to go off the rails. Time stops. Nothing in the world and nothing outside that little room mattered.

There was the terrible, helpless longing to pull back the past like a blanket and keep the present and the future at bay. How could anything take my Kris away?

I had always talked about my priorities being God, family, and career, in that order—a neat, orderly list. Deep down, I always knew my actions told a different story. But in one moment, life sorted things out, and everything was where it should have been. I needed God desperately, because only He could save my family. And career mattered less than some piece of trivia.

I fired off e-mails to those I cared about, promising to keep them informed. I'll share a few of them.

⊷

Sunday, March 29, 2009

Friends,

I've been able to reach a few of you regarding Kris' medical situation, and have appreciated your prayers.

There is no easy way to put this.

On Friday, we received a very difficult diagnosis from Mayo Clinic that Kris has liver cancer. The prognosis is not good.

I flew to Denver yesterday to bring our little Sarah home, and now we have our family all together, which is a blessing beyond measure. We return to Mayo Monday/Tuesday for additional biopsies and tests to determine whatever medical options we may have going forward.

We believe in miracles. We are praying for one and know that you will join us in that. Jesus is the Great Physician and in God all things are possible. We know that this is not God's will that Kris is sick. But we live in a fallen world where indeed "bad things happen to very good people."

We also know that God's circumstantial will prevails and makes good out of bad to accomplish His ultimate will. He always wins. Always.

Although we find ourselves badly bent, indeed we are not broken. This has been an extraordinary test of our faith and an opportunity to experience the "peace that surpasses all understanding."

Jesus said, "My grace is sufficient and my power is made perfect in your weakness." We are leaning on that promise and finding great comfort in its wonderful truth. Getting cancer was always Kris' greatest fear and now, facing the reality, she finds herself not the least bit terrified or angry. None of us are, but we are, of course, saddened to a level we never knew existed.

We truly believe in the power of prayer and give great thanks for having such a wonderful family of praying friends whom we know love us and will continue praying in this time of great need. We covet them.

We know that this is a long and very difficult road ahead. We are living totally in the moment, and one day at a time, which is a blessing in and of itself. We are not alone in this, and we're finding rest and peace in the reality of the promises of Jesus.

We hope to remain largely "unplugged" and present (another blessing in disguise) but promise to keep you updated from time to time.

Appreciate all prayers.

Ward, Kris, Andy, Michael, and Sarah Brehm

➤

I also called Andy and Mike, our two sons, when we were ready to return from Mayo. They were waiting for us with a fresh bouquet of flowers. The sight of my two sons wrapping Kris in their arms as they sobbed on our living room sofa was a sight beautiful and heartbreaking. Rarely are there moments when adult children and their parents share such unrestrained emotions together.

We had led, from the observation of friends, a "charmed life" as a family. Now everything was shattered. I stared straight ahead into a future that wouldn't include my wife and best friend of thirty years. I'd always known this kind of news would be hard—I just never imagined *how* hard. Suddenly, all the memories, all the routines, and all the ten thousand little pieces of a life together were broken. Marriage is a sum vastly, infinitely greater than the tiny pieces that make it up. When the news comes, each of those pieces—a song you both like, the way you share breakfast—are precious jewels you can't bear to lose. The little frictions and the tiny irritations, on the other hand, become utterly irrelevant.

And you learn what it is to pray without ceasing. Once my mind had wandered during prayer. Not now. I was forced to my knees, totally focused on pleading my case before God. Then, somewhere in the midst of that dark night of the soul, you experience what Paul calls "the peace of God, which transcends all understanding" (Philippians 4:7). Together the four of us felt it, the greatest of miracles.

What about those famous stages of grief? We skipped some of them: anger, despair, denial, and fear. Somehow, we came down hard on acceptance. We didn't know how, but things were going to be all right. We felt the soft voice of Jesus saying, "Do not let your hearts be troubled" (John 14:27). I felt this was the first true, severe test of my faith.

Later, people would even say Kris "glowed"—and she did. Everyone noticed the strength and the joy she had. What they didn't know was that cancer had been her deepest fear. She had watched her mother, at fifty-two, succumb to it slowly and mercilessly. This had been the one dread she carried, but what she felt instead of terror was the reality of God's presence. She bore testimony to the fact that Jesus still calms storms.

It occurred to me that the word *faith* is a weak and benign word, at least as we use it. The real thing is powerful beyond words. And *trust* only raised a deep question for me. If someone had asked me a few weeks earlier if I *trusted* Jesus, I'd tentatively said, "I think so." In reality, I tended to trust my personal efforts. But those efforts could do nothing now. It took this event for me to understand that, yes, I did trust Jesus, because now I had tested it out. I'd brought Him the greatest burden ever to be placed on my shoulders—and He'd taken the full load.

A miracle came. Only days after we came home, word came that a surgeon had been found who was willing to attempt the nearly impossible surgery. His name was Dr. Nagorney.

◆━━◆

Saturday, April 4, 2009

Friends,

Thank you for the outpouring of love, heartfelt notes, and, most importantly, the prayers for Kris. Here's an update.

We spent most of this last week at Mayo Clinic for a biopsy of Kris' liver, multiple MRIs, and a battery of other tests ordered by the specialists in Rochester. While we were told initially that surgery wasn't an option, we got a call Friday af-

ternoon from Kris' primary attending physician, Dr. Lewis Roberts, with the good news the head of surgery specializing in liver, Dr. David Nagorney, felt that it might be possible.

We plan on going back down to Mayo Clinic Wednesday/ Thursday for various pre-surgery tests and to meet with the surgeons to get their assessment of risks/rewards. Surgery would be April 17 or sooner. They'd first perform an exploratory probe of her abdomen, and if the cancer hasn't spread, they'd attempt to remove the cancer that has been limited to the right lobe of her liver. Having no treatment options initially, we are claiming this as a great gift from God, who has renewed our hope.

Please pray for her physicians at Mayo. In addition to Doctors Lewis and Nagorney, the team will include her surgeon, Dr. Robert Stanhope, and oncologist, Dr. Steve Alberts.

We are also so grateful that Kris hasn't yet experienced any pain or discomfort. ... In fact, as we write this, she is taking yet another lap around the lakes. Throughout this terrible ordeal, the Lord has shown His wondrous hand to us in a number of ways.

Kris' primary physician at Mayo is considered one of the world's leading experts on liver cancer. His schedule initially was too full to fit us in, but we were somehow able to see him last Friday, and he is now quarterbacking the care for Kris.

It turns out that he is from Ghana and was discipled by our missionary friends, Dave and Sherry Hall in Accra, years ago. Small world, indeed.

While sitting anxiously as Dr. Roberts told us, much to my dismay, about the upcoming tests Kris would have to un-

dergo, she and I, completely independent of one another, jotted down Romans 12: "Be patient in affliction." Glancing at each other's paper, we realized we had written the same thing and underlined it three times.

And when meeting with another one of Kris' physicians, Dr. Robert Stanhope, he noticed my Bible and asked if I was a pastor. It turns out he too is a follower of Jesus and has performed volunteer surgery in Kenya. He put his arms around Kris and me and said a beautiful prayer. He has seen and believes in miracles.

Kris received a call from President George W. Bush on Friday, and they talked for over fifteen minutes about faith in trials. He promised, and she received this morning via overnight mail, a copy of a book he is reading, The Reason for God *by Timothy Keller.*

God is faithful.

We thank you from the bottom of our hearts for your love and prayers.

Those prayers have indeed been "the tiny nerves that move the mighty hand of God," and have been felt by our family. Keep them coming!

With great thanks and confidence that our God will see us through,

Ward, Kris, Andy, Michael, and Sarah Brehm

◆━━◆

We would find out much later that Dr. Stanhope had called Dr. Nagorney and asked him to review the MRI results. Kris was surely going to die in a matter of weeks, he said—why not at least try? Dr. Nagorney's nickname at Mayo is "The Wizard."

⊢⊣

Saturday, April 11, 2009

Friends,

We've been given the green light for surgery this coming Friday, April 17.

The plan is to first perform a staging laparoscopy, which will provide actual pictures and additional biopsies to be able to determine exactly if the cancer has spread. ... Fortunately, the tumor has not affected the lobe of the liver, so the doctors are confident it can function properly. If all goes well, Kris will be hospitalized for about a week and then will be home recuperating.

Our family will spend the night before the surgery in Rochester, celebrating Sarah's twentieth birthday. She has taken a leave of absence from her studies at the University of Denver to be home with her mom and family.

Last Sunday, our pastor, Dr. Arthur Rouner, who confirmed both Kris and me when we were fifteen, came to our house for prayer and anointed Kris with oil per the healing instructions of James. Steve Moore has led a Bible study for our extended family the last two Saturday mornings. Last week we looked at Luke 10, and this week we dove into the passion play of Luke 23. It's been a wonderful sanctuary and time of prayer and learning.

Angels continue to be encamped and stand guard all around us. We've been filled with awe and thanks for the way we've been lifted up by grace and the prayers of so many. We find ourselves at the "deep end of the pool," and obviously, we're filled with deep sadness, yet we've been protected thus far from fear, anger, and dismay.

We believe in miracles and continue to pray for one. We believe in healing, and we pray that Kris will be healed. Above all, we believe in Jesus as the Great Physician, and have placed this burden into the best hands of all—His.

With heartfelt thanks for your prayers, love, and support. Happy Easter!

The Brehm Family

◆—◆

Friday, April 17, 2009

We bring good news from the Mayo Clinic in Rochester, Minnesota.

Kris' surgery was considerably more complicated than originally anticipated. The operation began at 11:40 a.m. and concluded at 7:00 p.m. In addition to two surgeons, there were twenty-four assisting nurses and technicians.

The laparoscopy allowed the operation to commence. Dr. Stanhope was successful with Kris' hysterectomy and also in removing two cancerous growths in her pelvis and abdomen, as well as 67 lymph nodes and gallbladder. Dr. Nagorney was able to remove an enormous tumor in her liver that was as large as a basketball and weighed nine and a half pounds. The size and position of the tumor made the surgery extremely difficult and took extraordinary skill and experience.

But we have now met with both surgeons, and they are in agreement that all visible cancer has been removed. Due to the length and complicated nature of the multiple operations, Kris will spend the next few days under close supervision in intensive care ... a week or so.

We give great thanks for these physicians considered to be among the very best in the world! And, above all, we praise God from whom all blessings flow.

Before the surgery, Dr. Stanhope met with us and we prayed together for the surgical team's wisdom, discernment, and skill. Those prayers were answered in spades. We were also provided a wonderful set of meditations based on the Beatitudes that were a blessing throughout this difficult day.

You may recall that, a week ago Thursday, we were given the prognosis that surgery was not an option and nothing could be done for Kris. We have now been given hope where none could be found before. When something that is impossible happens, by definition it's a miracle. We claim God has done a wonderful one today. The many prayers from across the world have been answered in the way we hoped they would. This is a powerful testimony to the greatest physician of all, Jesus.

We remain committed to taking things day by day; we're far from out of the woods. The ongoing challenges regarding future prognosis and treatment choices remain daunting, but we have great hope (translated from Greek as "confident expectation") that our faith in God's provision and the fervent prayers from friends like you will see us through.

With great thanks and rejoicing,

The Brehm Family

◆━◆

Miracles are, by definition, extraordinarily rare. Some have insisted Kris was saved because of our strong faith, but we're certain that's not true. Indeed, the very best people in all of Scripture, those with the strongest faith, ended up suffering terribly and losing their lives. We know so many who have not survived, and we've grieved with their families.

So, we acknowledge this miracle as we think we should—a profound and incomprehensible heavenly mystery.

◆━◆

Thursday, April 24, 2009

Friends,

After a week at the Mayo Clinic, we're grateful to be home. Kris had a great week of recovery, and we're so thankful for the competent and compassionate caregivers in Rochester.

We learned this week that had the tumor not been removed, it would have caused her death within weeks. These doctors saved her life, and we thank God.

We're happy to report that Kris is feeling well and in no pain. Her liver has already recovered 70 percent of its function—despite having over half of it removed.

After a week of studying the biopsies, the doctors still haven't been able to pinpoint the exact source of the cancer. Leave it to Kris to confound the best diagnostic teams in the world! There was never any doubt in our minds that God was with us, but His presence has been confirmed each step of the way on this road we find ourselves walking.

We were also reminded of the ten blind men to whom Jesus gave sight. Only one of them returned to say thank you. We'll never lose sight of the many miracles—large and small—the Lord has already done. We'll never forget to say thank you. Perhaps the greatest "privilege" of this problem is a certainty of faith and the undeniable presence of the Holy Spirit.

Kris is putting all of her energy into recovery now, and today's verse was appropriate: "Do not worry about tomorrow, for tomorrow will worry about itself. Each day has enough trouble of its own." We've been strengthened by this adversity. We're prepared for the difficulties that lie ahead, knowing we're in the Lord's hands. Again, we thank all of you, our family of friends, for your prayers, notes, concern, love, and support.

The Brehm Family

Thursday, May 5, 2009

We returned to Mayo Clinic twice last week for additional procedures and CT scans. Dr. Stanhope reminded us last week in a note that the real credit needs to go to God, because given the circumstances and challenges, only God could have guided the circumstances and process. Amen.

Mayo has finally diagnosed the primary source of Kris' cancer: her right fallopian tube. The original cancer was less than one-eighth of one inch in diameter. Fallopian tube cancer is extremely rare, and so is her case. Kris is considered to be cancer-free for now. We thank God!

We continue to pray the way forward regarding the suggested chemotherapy regiment of carboplatin and Taxol. The hope is to rid the body of any microscopic cancer cells that may still exist. This would decrease the likelihood of the cancer ever returning. We ask for your continued prayers for healing and for the cancer not to return.

Kris is now taking short walks. As part of her healing regimen, she has incorporated acupuncture, massage, and nutritional counsel.

Our entire family wants to thank all of you for your love and concern. We've been lavished with much kindness: home-made dinners, a surprise birthday party, a handmade quilt and prayer shawl, a charm bracelet filled with memories, a landscape of flowers, five hundred e-mails, and countless cards and voicemail messages. We've constantly been uplifted, seeing God's goodness through all of you.

Most precious of all were your prayers. From Minnesota as well as all over the United States; from the rural pastors of Ethiopia; the nomadic friends in West Pokot, Kenya; all throughout Africa; and around the world—prayers have been launched and answered by God.

With heartfelt thanks,

The Brehm family

P.S. Our updates will become less frequent, so please consider no news as good news, and please keep up the prayers as we move forward.

Kris' Story, Part 2: Overtime

When Each New Day Is a Gift

> Oh yes—God takes pleasure in your pleasure!
> Dress festively every morning. Don't skimp on colors
> and scarves. Relish life with the spouse you love, each and
> every day of your precarious life. Each day is God's gift.
> It's all you get in exchange for the hard work of staying alive.
> Make the most of each one!
>
> —ECCLESIASTES 9:7–9 (MSG)

Kris needed three months of chemotherapy. One friend termed it a "mop-up operation." Like cancer itself, chemo was another fear Kris had carried for years. The poison meant to save her life dripped into her veins. Yet she had no ill effects at all. She did lose her hair, but she walked every day—and she continued to glow.

Following the chemo came our realization that for at best five years, we'd live with uncertainty and regular testing. Now was the time for those inevitable thoughts: *Why us?*

At certain moments, we did ponder that question. But with it came a fresh perspective: Why *not* us if *someone* had to face these things?

Kris had no job on which a family was dependent. And for that matter, I had the ability to walk away from mine as needed.

What if this had happened to a single mother of small children somewhere?

On top of that, Kris was supposed to have died; it was a medical certainty. Our thinking was now set on the truth that she was living in overtime. New birthdays and summers at the cabin—these were *gifts*, enjoyed without the ill effects so many experience with chemo. When each new day is seen as a gracious blessing, life becomes fresh and an occasion for gratitude. This is what the gamblers call "playing on house money."

The Scriptures call on us to be thankful in all circumstances. We found that to be a command we could follow with enthusiasm.

❧

Wednesday, May 27, 2009

Friends,

It has been just over two months since we first learned of Kris' cancer, and we continue to marvel, along with the doctors at Mayo, at how God has worked a miracle.

Kris' stage-four fallopian tube cancer, which had spread to her liver and isolated lymph nodes, is almost always fatal. But we've been reminded time and time again by her doctors that her case is unique, because the surgeons were able to remove all the cancer in Kris they could see. That's very seldom possible.

We've been back down to Rochester a number of times over the last few weeks, due to some complications with swelling, as well as for additional CT scans and a battery of blood tests. But Kris is feeling good for the first time in a long while.

After much thought and prayer, Kris has agreed to follow the advice of Dr. Alberts, Dr. Nagorney, and Dr. Stanhope and undergo chemotherapy, which will minimize the chances of any microscopic cancer cells returning. The prescribed chemotherapy regimen of carboplatin and Taxol will be given six times (once every three weeks) over the course of the next four months.

Kris will begin the chemotherapy tomorrow under the direction of Dr. John Seng at Minnesota Oncology, in the Virginia Piper Cancer Clinic. This is a scary step for Kris, the realization of a long-held fear. This will also be difficult given that she is just now starting to feel "normal," having mostly recovered from her April surgery. It's hard for her to contemplate the chance of a new physical challenge due to the chemotherapy. Nor does she look forward to losing her beautiful blonde hair. Please pray for her strength of mind and body, as well as for minimal side effects or impact on her energy and spirit.

We know we can't predict the future. But deep down, we always thought these were things that happened to other people. Now we're learning to take life day by day, minute by minute. We find delight and give thanks for just having Kris alive and with us.

Again, we want to thank the hundreds of people from near and far who have been so faithful in prayer. We ask you to continue. Pray the cancer will not come back and for complete and total healing. Those prayers are the tiny nerves that can move the mighty hand of God. So far, they've done so magnificently.

Thank you. Thank you. Thank you.

◆━◆

Friday, June 25, 2009

We haven't provided an update—no news has been good news. Kris is doing extremely well, and the doctors continue to be impressed by her strength, attitude, and recovery. She completed her second chemotherapy session June 19, and we celebrate her being one-third of the way through the six-course regimen. Her last treatment (yahoo!) will be on September 8.

Our collective prayers have been answered: Kris has not suffered any of the nastier side effects of the chemotherapy. Other than being pretty tired the first few days after the infusions, Kris has felt fine. She's had no aching, nausea, or "tingling" yet; the doctors say this is a strong sign that she may dodge many of the side effects going forward.

They do say the fatigue will be cumulative, but with Kris' energy and outlook, nobody is betting on a major slowdown. She's losing her hair, which, although a little unsettling, we take as a sign that the drugs are working exactly as they should. In two weeks, she'll have a comprehensive CT scan to confirm that the cancer has not returned.

We were amazed to learn that these chemotherapy drugs stay in her system for only twenty-four hours. They attack and destroy new, rapidly growing cells. So, while this medicine kills microscopic cancer cells, it also reduces her white cell blood count. This makes Kris more susceptible to infection throughout the course of each treatment.

We're also celebrating Kris' total recovery from major surgery. She's taking long walks and is again busy around the house. This last Saturday, the day following the latest chemotherapy, she led the way as we went on a ten-mile round-

trip bike ride from our cabin to Crosslake! Her weight, strength, and color have all returned, in addition to her always energetic and optimistic outlook. She made her famous homemade strawberry pie for Father's Day. In a word, "She's back!"

A few days ago, I reread all our updates since we first learned of this cancer. I was again both amazed and grateful for the way that God has been with us each step of the way. While we rejoice in her amazing recovery from that "hopeless" original prognosis, we thank God even more for our being able to personally experience His closeness, faithfulness, and presence in both the darkest hours as well as the joyful ones on this unfamiliar road on which we find ourselves.

While Kris is technically cancer-free, the cancer can return. But God has given us a certainty of faith that gives us confident expectation that, no matter what the next few weeks, months, and years may bring, we are indeed not alone in this. We've declared victory.

We'll never forget or stop giving thanks to the Lord, who has answered our collective prayers so visibly and powerfully.

Every blessing in Him,

The Brehm Family

◆━◆

Monday, September 21, 2009

Dear Friends,

During these 178 days, we've experienced the beauty of living day by day. We're thankful for the love of our family and our ability to experience and express unconditional love for one another in a whole new way. We're thankful for all of you, our friends who have been so faithful in your love, concern, and prayers—for the encouraging notes and visits that "just happened" to arrive when we needed them most!

Above all, we're thankful to the Lord for His faithfulness regardless of what challenges lie ahead. We're thankful for His peace (in the storm) and for being with us in what has been an almost surreal adventure in faith.

Blessings, thanks, and love,

The Brehm family

❧

Sunday, September 27, 2009

Good news! Kris completed her last of six chemotherapy sessions on September 11. Other than sporting a cute bald head, Kris was blessed with none of the negative side effects of chemotherapy.

We've also received fantastic news regarding her recent medical tests. The new CT scan and blood work show no sign of cancer. Hallelujah!

Kris will begin having a CT scan and lab tests every three months for the next few years, watching for cancer. We've been told the first two years are particularly important; after five years, she would be technically "cured." We're claiming this already!

Given all this good news, we plan to go to Australia, God willing, in late October. Sarah is studying at Bond University near the Gold Coast, and we will travel together for two and a half weeks "down under."

Since the first day of Kris' diagnosis, a good friend of our family has sent an e-mail each day with an encouraging passage from Scripture. We have attached it below because it's Kris' favorite passage. She committed it to memory six years ago; it's been comforting throughout this journey.

> *Rejoice in the Lord always. I will say it again: Rejoice! Let your gentleness be evident to all. The Lord is near. Do not be anxious about anything, but in everything, by prayer and petition, with thanksgiving, present your requests to God. And the peace of God, which transcends all understanding, will guard your hearts and your minds in Christ Jesus. Finally, brothers and sisters, whatever is true, whatever is noble, whatever is right, whatever is pure, whatever is lovely, whatever is admirable—if anything is excellent or praiseworthy—think about such things. (Philippians 4:4–9)*

◆━◆

Sunday, May 16, 2010

It has been more than eight months since our last update.

We'll start out by saying Kris skied fifty days this past winter on her Telluride season pass. She spent most of her time on black and double-black diamond runs and volunteering with Telluride's adaptive ski program for those with disabilities. Kris has been able to return to running and to her normal, active life. She sports a bit of an unusual hair style, but we're grateful for each and every strand!

Dr. Alberts, Kris' oncologist, reminds us (unnecessarily) that Kris is a miracle. For just over a year, she has been cancer-free. In the blood test, the CA 125 tumor marker, anything less than

35 is classified as normal. When Kris was first diagnosed, she was at 945. This last week she scored a 7.

God has granted us "the peace that surpasses all understanding," guarding our hearts from anxiety, anger, denial, and the usual emotions of adversity. Another gift has been realizing the distinction between merely "having faith" and being able to trust Jesus, regardless of outcome.

We remain thankful in all circumstances. So thankful for all of your support, love, and continued prayers.

Blessings to you and yours,

The Brehm Family

◆━◆

Yet another gift was that we learned not to sweat the small stuff—and that nearly *all* of it was small stuff. When we found ourselves perplexed or in disagreement, we'd say, "Well, it isn't cancer."

Medically, we weren't out of the woods yet, of course. We continued to go down to Mayo every four months for lab tests, keeping an eye out for cancer. A close friend coined a phrase for what we felt that week: *scanxiety.* It was a surreal experience to have to wait for the results, knowing how high the stakes were. This *wasn't* "the small stuff." When that door handle turned and the doctor came in, it was another referendum on life or death.

I was never good at living life one day at a time, but now we found ourselves living four months at a time. In the grip of "scanxiety" during the checkups at Mayo, we always experienced joy and relief when Dr. Alberts gave us the thumbs-up in that familiar ninth-floor waiting room.

Then, in May 2013, on the one-year anniversary of the diagnosis, Dr. Alberts told us to go home and not to come back for a *whole year.* No interim tests; no "scanxiety."

We went home and enjoyed every detail of life.

On May 29, 2014, Kris was tested again. The staid and steady
Dr. Alberts came in and looked like someone else. His eyes were
dancing and his smile was expansive. "Perfect!" he exclaimed,
referring to the lab results, and gave Kris a huge hug. "The cancer
is gone, and it's not coming back!"

Tears. Joy. *Thanks.* It was as powerful a moment as the one
when we heard the bad news—but the very reversal of it.

Gone. Cured.

On the way home, I composed one last e-mail to our wonderful friends.

◆—◆

Thursday, May 29, 2014

It's been five years since Kris' cancer diagnosis. With joy-filled hearts, we want to share that she is officially pronounced cured.

The Mayo physicians—by now our dear friends as well as our doctors—acknowledge that we are the recipients of a miracle. It is very humbling. And the reason behind this blessing remains a deep mystery. So many we know are grieving their loss of loved ones, while others are currently in the throes of battling major medical ailments.

We are thankful—thankful for your love and prayers through these years, for the expert medical care, and, above all, to God for a miracle we will never fully comprehend. So, we have the privilege of living today's verse from Isaiah 55:12:

> *You will go out in joy and be led forth in peace;*
> *the mountains and hills will burst into song before you,*
> *and all the trees of the field will clap their hands.*

Amen indeed!

The Brehm Family

━━

As the normally calm, businesslike Dr. Alberts failed to contain his joy while giving us that last good news, his smiling face melting away our icy tension, Kris asked him, "You don't get this a lot, do you?"

"No," he said. "Hardly ever. We can treat the cancer and pray it remains in remission, but very seldom are we able to use that wonderful word—*cure.*"

All we can do is stop contemplating the mystery and start enjoying it to the fullest. We think of those faithful, loving friends—the one, for example, who wrote prayers and shared Scriptures each day for Kris, only to lose his lovely wife to a similar cancer. Or even Kris' sister, Karla, who was recently diagnosed with a rare form of it herself. Will the miracle arrive for her? We can't know.

Many of our friends have lost wives and mothers. The prayers were answered in the affirmative for us, but again, our only response can be unquestioning gratitude—and *anything* but pride. Our faith is no stronger, nor our lives any better, than most of these people. Jesus said that our Father sends rain on the righteous and the unrighteous.

For that reason, it's also true that our present joy is merely a respite. The rains will come eventually. Grief and pain are inseparable from living. To know God is to embrace mystery. His wisdom is beyond us.

These things remind us of God's greatness, of the fragility of life, and of the urgency of living this day for all it's worth.

By the way, as of this writing, Kris has been totally cured from cancer and is no longer required to go back to Mayo. She will most certainly die someday, hopefully a long way off, but not from this cancer. For that, I am forever grateful.

25

Nobody's Getting Out of Here Alive

The Only Thing Certain about Life Is Death

I'm not afraid to die—
I just don't want to be there when it happens.
—WOODY ALLEN

No matter how rich you become, how famous
or powerful, when you die the size of your funeral
will still pretty much depend on the weather.
—MICHAEL PRITCHARD

Through the past five years, I've gotten just an inkling of how Job, the biblical character, felt. From a medical perspective, it's been one thing piled on top of another.

First, I was diagnosed with polycythemia vera, an exceedingly rare but currently benign form of blood cancer. Thankfully, we've kept it under control with an oral chemotherapy regimen with few side effects.

A year after my polycythemia vera diagnosis, at Mayo Clinic, I was diagnosed as a Type 1 diabetic, which again was extraordinarily rare, especially for someone approaching sixty. Then, at sixty-two, I was diagnosed with an aggressive form of prostate cancer that required surgery—and again, we were thankful the operation was a success.

To top it off, I had a follow-up CT scan and related blood tests, indicating that I also have chronic lymphoma leukemia. The latter, thankfully, is currently indolent (i.e., sluggish). Hopefully it will stay slow and sluggish for a long, long time.

Thus far, I'm batting a thousand against these challenges. So why the pity party?

These events do get me thinking. My internist and good friend from the University of Minnesota, Dr. Greg Vercellotti, attempted to advise me regarding the prostate surgery. He asked my hematologist—also a good friend—how long he thought I had to live. When he told me his question, I pressed him for the answer he received. To be honest, I'd never pondered my own life expectancy.

He was very reluctant to reply, as it was only a wild guess based upon the medical facts. I said I understood all that, and I still wanted to know the number.

Ten years.

I took the answer and thought it over for a while, finally deciding I had little to complain about. I guess the way I saw it, anything less than a decade would seem a bit stingy on God's part. Anything more would be a bonus. Basically, if I really had ten years, I was breaking even.

But there's no way to hear such a compelling opinion about your life—and death—without launching into other rumination you'd normally never approach. For example: What if that ten-year number was a firm figure after all, instead of a guess? None of us know the day or the hour, but just as an intellectual exercise: What if life were as precisely timed as a football game, and God gave me the "ten-year warning"? How would I do things differently? Or *would* I do things differently?

It didn't take me long to answer that question: yes! It would change a lot of things for me. Knowing when the clock would tick down would make me very methodical; it would have to. The next question was harder, however: *How* would it change things? What would I do with my precisely timed ten years?

I took the question seriously enough to write down a ten-year plan. As I was thinking it through, I called Doug Coe, my dear friend and mentor in the nation's capital, for help. As I told him about my ten-year plan, he was intrigued, and he asked me to come to Washington to see him and discuss it further.

We met at the Cedars, a beautiful mansion on the Potomac River, donated for the purpose of hosting leaders and praying friends from all across the world. It was a cheerful setting for a rather grim conversation. After embracing in a big hug and exchanging various pleasantries, we sat down and got to business.

"So, Ward, I want to hear more about this ten-year plan of yours. Have you put anything to paper yet? And if so, did you bring it along?"

"Yes," I replied, reaching into my coat pocket and pulling out my six-page outline.

"Well, that's tremendous," Doug said. "Here, hand it over and let me take a peek."

I handed the document to Doug, eager for him to review all the judgments I'd made about how to use my time. Without breaking eye contact with me or losing his smile, he neatly shredded my careful essay into tiny bits of paper, then proceeded to throw the remains into the wastebasket. I stared incredulously.

"It's the most ridiculous idea I've ever heard," he said. "A ten-year plan—really? Ward, what you need is a three-*day* plan!"

"But—"

"Here's what I want you to do, Ward. Imagine you have three days left to live—then make *that* plan. Keep following it for as many days as you live on this earth."

As usual, Doug was right. As long as I've known him, he's been able to pull the absolutely correct answer out of the air and put it in front of me. And I knew this was one more of those occasions.

I sat and began to see everything through this new lens, realizing that if I had three days to live, I'd bring my family around me and tell them how much I loved them. I'd teach my children the most crucial lessons of my own life experiences, not wasting a second.

And really, that's why you're reading the book in your hands.

I want to be perfectly clear and establish that all those medical issues I listed are indolent. They're sleepy, lazy, inactive. Normally, I don't approve of those traits, but when it comes to my medical challenges, I encourage their sluggishness. I don't hurry them along at all. They may remain that way for many, many years, and I may even outlive *you*!

Still, the ten-year window in my mind isn't as easily shredded as that sheet of paper was. It lives on in my imagination, and I did decide to keep exploring it academically.

Jeff Bird, my business partner, confidant, and friend, put me in my place spiritually, as he often does. (As you've noticed by now, I have a strong support staff of experts in the art of putting me in my place.) Over a casual lunch some time back, Jeff said, "You know what, Ward? I've been thinking, and we actually have very little time left to sacrifice."

I simply gave him a quizzical look, because I wasn't following at all.

"Well, think about it," he said. "When we die, we go to heaven. In heaven, there will be no more suffering, no more pain, and thus no more opportunity to serve Jesus—or the people here on earth He wants us to serve."

I had never even remotely considered that proposition, but after pondering it for a bit, I realized he was right. Heaven is "within eternity," but every moment on earth is a precious commodity. As it passes, it's gone forever. *We get exactly one shot at every passing moment.* So, the question becomes: How should I best make use of this hypothetical ten-year window?

For starters, I would need to be more intentional about my

actions. When I was young, I was immortal—or at least that's how I felt. But given our cultural philosophy, even in middle age I had failed to take my mortality with any degree of seriousness.

I remember having lunch with my friend and mentor Wheelock Whitney. In the middle of our conversation, he interrupted and said, "Ward, I have something very serious to tell you."

I fell silent and regarded him with a sense of foreboding.

He said, "I have a terminal disease."

Needless to say, I was shocked. I leaned across the table and grabbed both his hands. "My God, Wheelock, what is it?"

"I'm eighty-five years old. I never imagined I would live even this long, but how long do I have left? A couple years? Five? Ten at most? You see, I'm *terminal*," he said with a wry smile.

Sure enough, Wheelock ended up living another four vibrant years and remains a model for me on not just how to live but also how to die and how to "finish well." And he lived his last years to their absolute fullest.

Our culture lives in denial regarding death. It's an abstract thought that only impacts others—until it impacts us. And it will, of course, without exception.

Thinking "in the finite" has become an interesting exercise. Life can be looked at the way we would look at, say, a package of gourmet coffee from across the world that we couldn't restock. With every cup, we know the supply is closer to running out. So we try to savor every sip.

Christmas comes, and I don't think of it as one in an endless line of these holidays. I see it as one in a limited series of ten. Ten summers at the lake. Ten of my children's birthdays. How does that change things? It has made me more intentional, more prone to living in the present. Africa helped me learn that lesson. Aging and Kris' cancer have underlined it.

Perhaps more importantly, I've realized the danger of "self-pity syndrome." When it came to my own trials and tribulations, it was natural and normal—and I believe, acceptable—to briefly ask the "Why me?" question when answers were simply not evident. But more significantly, prolonged self-pity is an extremely slippery slope that bottoms out in bitterness. And that's a truly wretched place to end up.

As I contemplated how I would live under a ten-year limit, the first practical response hit me immediately: I needed to leave the company I founded forty years ago.

I've always lived in dread of the word *retirement*. For me, it carried a world of negative connotations: an intentional downgrade to irrelevancy. So, in the interest of avoiding an unpleasant word, I say I'm inspired rather than retired.

I want to be inspired based on the point Jeff made. God gave me a calling and a limited amount of time for addressing it. But that doesn't mean going into a frantic rush to achieve goals. Actually, it means training myself to slow down, be more thoughtful, and pray much more in order to be able to discern the still, small voice of God's calling.

A friend told me that some years ago, there was a survey of fifty people at least ninety-five years old. They were asked what they would do differently if they had life to live again. Three answers predominated in their replies:

- They would risk more.
- They would reflect more.
- They would do more things that would live on after they were gone.

I have a good way to go until age ninety-five, but I understand what they're saying. When life has a limit—as it most definitely does—I feel no need to play it safe. I can take risks. I can stop and smell the roses. And I can put my effort into a legacy, so I can feel good about the investment that is my life.

Kris' cancer and my own challenges have helped me embrace the idea of letting go and trusting Jesus completely. But can I be "all in"? That's a little harder. I know it means picking up my cross and following Him—and that means sacrificing my desires for those of Jesus. It's hard, it's daily, and it can't be done without help and encouragement.

So, I've begun to try and live accordingly. Now five years on, the hypothetical clock should be reading five to go, but I have a way of letting it be a moving target—in other words, with each year that passes, I add the year back and figure I still have ten to go. I asked my hematologist, Greg, about it the other day and he gave the thumbs-up. The point is not the total, because it's only a guess anyway—it's how I live right now, knowing the clock is running.

I try always to remember that having adequate time and resources is an extraordinary blessing. It's the freedom to choose the right way. But I also feel a powerful responsibility to my calling and believe I'll be held accountable. It's a dilemma only a very fortunate man might face, as opposed to most in this world who struggle for the next meal. Nevertheless, I feel that dilemma as I seek to determine what is truly important for the unspecified time that remains for me.

I think I often take my life and eventual death way too seriously. All the things I think are mine will be gone. Someone else will take over "my" favorite pew at church. My beautiful clothes will be given or thrown away. All my treasure will soon be second-hand junk. Though my family will be temporarily brokenhearted and my close friends sad, "this too shall pass" rather quickly.

Tony Campolo once said something to the effect of, "Just remember that after you die, they are going to take you out to the cemetery, throw you in a hole, and cover you with dirt before going back to the church and eating chicken salad!" That helps with my perspective.

In our Tuesday morning prayer group, one of the members shared with us the tragedy of having his beloved wife of many years die in his arms while she was in her midfifties. The story was as moving as it was tragic, and there wasn't a dry eye in the room. It was quite a sight to see twelve grown men—many of them "captains of industry"—openly weeping at 7:30 a.m.

Our friend paused as we reflected with deep emotion on his words. Then he said, "I'm very moved by your sadness, which I accept as an expression of your love for me. But the most important thing I'll ever say to any of you is this: you'll all go through what I've experienced—each and every one of you. Be prepared."

Yup, one of the most amazing (yet well-known) statistics of all time is that one out of every one person dies. When people tell us—Kris and me—that we've dodged a bullet, I can only smile and say, "No, it's only been postponed a bit."

26

Growing Old

Reflecting as the Waterfall Grows Near

❖

To me, growing old is great.
It's the very best thing—considering the alternative.
—Michael Caine

You may not be as good as you used to be,
but you are for sure better than you are going to be.
—Yogi Berra

We hear about it all our lives. We see it happen to others. We know it lies ahead. Yet somehow it comes as some degree of surprise to find that we, too, are on a single voyage that must finally reach its destination.

The river winds along, the water is cool, we're just learning how to sit back and enjoy the ride—and then we hear the first sounds of the waterfall around the next bend. The question is, what will we do with that knowledge?

First, we need to think about it with greater honesty. I was discussing some aspect of what I called "middle age" when my daughter, Sarah, piped in, "So, Dad, do you really think you're going to live to be 126 years old?" Thanks, Sarah.

"Halftime" was over some time ago for me, and I need to accept that I may be well into the fourth quarter—though, as I shared in chapter 24, Kris considers herself to be in overtime.

Like many of my friends, I enjoyed a full and interesting career. I owned two insurance consulting companies. I realize my partners would suggest that a relatively small percentage of my time over the past ten years was actually spent working; still, I enjoyed the "platform" that came with being a business owner. I was relevant. I was "in the game."

When selling the business, I had to confront my fear of leaving that game and sitting on the bench—*being irrelevant*. But I also knew that my time and energy were increasingly moving toward Africa. And to me, that was more than a game. Large projects and objects of passion helped me face the prospect of walking away from my business career. Kris also helped, pointing out that business was a platform for the "first half" but that the second half should be about following my heart. Most business people, after all, retire during their sixties.

So, that's what I did. When I walked away, I went "cold turkey." I was done.

Then a good friend said something that gave me the shivers. He'd overheard his wife talk about what she anticipated for his retirement. "Well," she said, "he'll probably shuffle around in his robe and slippers all day."

Really?

That wasn't going to be me. Of that I was certain, and I've avoided it so far. I can honestly say I've never been more active, involved, or well utilized in my life. If anything, the challenge is finding the "robe and slippers" time I actually need.

Regardless, all around me are reminders of the reality of aging. I was talking with some buddies recently, for instance. We found it remarkable that so many of our young friends in the Twin Cities are now running some of the country's largest companies. Another good friend, one I perceived as being pretty young (same age as me, in other words), actually ran the country—they called him "forty-three."

Somehow, we never think of ourselves as old. Once, fifty-year-olds seemed old and crotchety. Now they seem like kids still wet behind the years. Bob Dylan once advised us never to trust anyone over thirty. I wonder how he's liking his wrinkles now that he's well over twice that age.

Kris and I were enjoying a dinner dance at a country club we hadn't frequented for a good while. We commented to each other about how many new "young people" were all around us. And we wondered about the whereabouts of all the "old people" we used to see. Then our eyes locked and we had the same thought: now *we're* the "old people." When did that happen? Without noticing it, we moved right into position and started playing our "old people" roles flawlessly.

Then there's my mother, who is ninety going on sixty. She's always fashionably dressed and looks and feels great. Once, someone asked her age, and she replied, "I'm sixty-seven."

My eyebrows shot up, and I glanced at her somewhat nervously. Was this the first sign she was becoming a little foggy? "Um, Mom—you're not sixty-seven. You're ninety-two."

"No, I'm not," she retorted. "I'm sixty-seven. I don't feel anything like ninety, so I'm going with sixty-seven. And by the way, how old do you feel?"

"Forty-seven," I said without missing a beat. "I don't feel sixty-three; I feel forty-seven."

I like that system. Take the test: how old do *you* feel?

Wheelock was sixty when I was forty, or thereabouts. We were having lunch, most of which consisted of me hearing his list of "What the heck?" issues. I listened blankly, and when he noticed my expression, he said, "Aw, you're way too young to understand. But you'll see. As you get older, things start to go wrong physically—and when they do, you tend to mutter, 'What the heck?'"

At the time, I just marked it off as a Wheelock thing. Then, no more than a week later, Kris and I were at a fine restaurant with dim lighting for romantic mood. As I studied the menu, I realized my arm was fully extended so I could read the type.

What the heck? I thought.

Later that month, I woke up in the middle of the night and realized I had to go to the bathroom—again—the same night! *What the heck?*

And there are a host of random aches and pains with seemingly no cause, relief, or cure, along with temporarily forgetting the names of people and places I've always known well. *What the heck?*

Another example is the way life picks up speed until the years fly by. I'm taking down the Christmas decorations when I realize I might as well leave them up—the next holiday season will leap upon us any moment now. How does that happen?

I went in for a routine eye exam and was told I need cataract surgery. I told the doctor I was confused—I thought cataract surgery was for old people. His silence made the point.

I've stopped saying I haven't seen someone for "a long time," because long times seem much shorter now. I call this my "double theory." That is, if I tell you I haven't seen someone in two years, the true number is four. If I say such-and-such took place five years ago, that means it was ten. I would swear my first trip to Africa was fifteen years ago—that's how it feels. But I know for a fact it was thirty. And I haven't been married for eighteen years, but thirty-six.

It can't be me; life stepped on the accelerator at some point.

Not long ago, I was in London with my son Andy, who was thirty-six. Traveling together as we were, I thought about the time I took our family on a month-long sabbatical to France. He was six years old then. I smiled thinking about that—and realized I was the age then that he is now! I thought a little more and realized six years later was the first African sojourn. Where did the time go? When did it start doling out years, one for the price of two?

I have to admit, however, that membership also has its privileges when it comes to the senior citizen club. It simply takes the maturing process of life to embrace those advantages. When I was in my thirties, I met up with a friend who'd just turned sixty-five. I couldn't curb my curiosity about how it must feel to be so ancient—so I asked.

"Great," he smiled. "I just do whatever I want now."

"That's good," I said. "But to be honest, it doesn't sound like anything that would be new for me. I'm already doing what I want."

"Ah—I see you don't know what I'm talking about." I gave him an inquiring look, and he added, "Okay. Christmas parties."

I kept staring.

"Well, do you go to a lot of Christmas parties?" he asked.

"Sure. Of course. Everybody does."

"Yeah, well everybody wants to be invited to every Christmas party. But the reality is that when it comes time to go to 'em, and it's snowing and cold outside, you wish you didn't have to go. So now, guess what? *I just don't go.* Don't have to."

I mulled that one over and realized it rang true. It felt like I was doing what I wanted, but, in fact, a whole lot of effort went into responding to the expectations of others. I made choices with less than healthy or honest ulterior motives. I performed. What I thought I wanted to do was, in actuality, what I felt obligated to do.

Now that I'm in the vicinity of that ripe old age, I'm going to fewer Christmas parties. Obligation and the opinions of others are no longer quite so crucial. Life is moving faster; I need to move slower. It's all good.

The disadvantages of aging, of course, are better known—starting with physical limitations. My knees, shoulders, and joints used to get along together great; we were a close-knit team, and now, when I call upon them, the "team members" grumble and often refuse to cooperate. If I require too much of them, they're sore with me. Even sleeping can be a pain in the neck!

I ran two marathons in my thirties; I sit them out now. Playing squash every workday for thirty years, plus tennis and paddle tennis—those days are gone too. I feel fortunate that I can still ski the extreme slopes in Telluride, but it's only a reminder that it's all downhill from here. The clock is ticking. Looking ahead, there's no looking back. How I face these things is what matters. My attitude is that it's great fun to focus on the quieter and gentler activities of fly fishing, golf, and hiking, all the while feeling grateful that I can still do those things while many can't.

My generation will think about and discuss nearly any subject other than that of growing older. We even avoid the word *death* by substituting euphemisms such as *passed on, went to a better place, joined the angels, departed, left our presence,* and so on. Some have said that *death* is today's ultimate obscenity. That's why we frantically try to look and feel young. I smile at seventy-five-year-old newscasters who show no wrinkles. Seriously, what's up with that?

Moms at the mall dress themselves like their teenage children. Where did all the yoga pants come from? Rock stars are still taking the stage pushing eighty, yet hanging onto shoulder-length hair and their 1960s wardrobes. We expected them to be rocking at this age, on the porch and in a chair with good back support. Wheelock reminded me recently that "eighty is the new eighty." Sometimes it is what it is.

I need to acknowledge aging and death, but that doesn't mean embracing them. I know what's inevitable. I think of Kris, the night before her life-and-death surgery at the Mayo Clinic—wanting a bike ride together. "This might be my last bike ride with you—ever," she said through her tears. It wasn't morbid, just realistic. She hadn't been given good odds, but she also didn't know a miracle was in store.

Could it be that my generation is so unaccepting of death because it doesn't understand a miracle is in store for all of us?

That a new life could be awaiting, one without painful joints, wrinkles, or tears of any kind?

A good friend of ours had his own encounter with major surgery. When we visited him in the hospital, he gave us a melancholy glance and said, "I'll never ride another horse again."

Kris quickly replied, "Why would you say that? You're making a reality out of a mere possibility. Why limit your future?"

She was right. It wasn't long before he was back in the saddle again.

Similarly, my pastor, Arthur Rouner, told me he'd taken his last trip to Africa. I took a page from Kris and challenged him on it. Maybe he could go back and maybe not, but the one way to settle the issue is to decide in advance on the negative. And again, I have a sneaking suspicion he'll be with me in Africa once again. A positive attitude is powerful medicine.

I've never understood why some people limit their horizons through pessimism. If we're going to speculate, why not set the bar as high as possible? I'll succumb to the aging process, but I won't go out without a fight. You might say death will never take me alive.

Sure, I know better things await me. Death is merely a change of address, hopefully to a better neighborhood. Still, I'm not done with the old neighborhood yet. My calling is inexhaustible until I'm too exhausted and call it a day. My wonderful wife, incredible children, and inspiring friends—all these are more than good company. I like living, and I'm not overly eager for the alternative. I guess I'm one of the many who want to go to heaven but aren't in a hurry to get there.

In my twenties and thirties, I attended lots of weddings and showers. In my sixties, I seem to honor the same cast of characters at their funerals, or at least visit them in the hospital. These are regular reminders of the inevitable, and they help me fend off delusions of immortality.

But even as I love my life, I'm becoming more holistic in

accepting the big picture. The morning after Kris was diagnosed with cancer, we talked quietly over breakfast. Tearfully, Kris told me she'd always planned on growing old together. Tears shone on our cheeks. One of the greatest blessings of my life, after hearing those words of love, has been God's kindness in letting it become a reality. Maybe without the cancer, we would have taken the gift for granted. As things stand, there's no way we can do anything but greet each new day with thanksgiving that we have that day together. No one but God could have given us both the reality and the joy we can now experience in that reality.

Today our prayer is to grow older with as much dignity, love, and grace as possible. I long to finish the race well. But that's a tall order when one can't clearly see the finish line. As life maintains its runaway velocity, I must hang on tight by being present in the moment. This time and this place must be my focus. It's the only way to slow down, but it's not easy. Every impulse is to launch our thoughts into the future, to let the mind wander somewhere else. A slow learning process leads to differentiating what is merely urgent from what is truly important. And I need to escape the cultural brainwashing that insists that busyness means significance. The word *no* needs to be a major player in my daily vocabulary, and I need to protect the margin that allows me to be still and *listen*. To God. To people I care about. To my own important reflections.

In reflection, I come to understand that for the better part of my life, I was intently focused on my résumé—my personal measuring stick of success and accomplishments. In that list of companies and honors lie my worth as a person, or so I assumed. I'm blessed by being free of that illusion now. I look back upon the old "thrill of the chase," and it looks less like a momentous quest and more like chasing my tail. I find myself thinking more about the unspoken eulogy. What was it all about? I know all good things come to an end—what matters now is to know that my life was about good things.

That means doing some careful and even merciless inventory. I finally came to the realization that my life was over capacity. Like an elevator, it can hold only a certain amount of weight before something very bad happens. I was busy, but I felt empty and weary rather than proud and important. My calendar showed a dizzying number of obligations and commitments to honor. Which I did. Then, having done so, I took the step of reserving a one-year sabbatical from saying yes to anything new, anything I wasn't already locked into. I needed one year of margin to take stock of the systems and approaches that were overloading my life (not to mention time to slow down, rest, and find new strength).

The real test came when my lips had to form the world's most powerful two-letter word: *no.* Friends were bewildered, even offended. Why couldn't I meet their request? I offered the truth as my defense: I regretted to disappoint them, but I was taking a much-needed sabbatical. The response was usually a moment of thought, and then, "What a great idea! I'm going to look into taking a sabbatical too!"

I see the future in a new way. Whereas once it was based on the youthful illusion of time as a bottomless well, now I'm grounded more in reality, on limits, and on the need for self-management and careful allotment of the moments given to me.

The past is a good place—a treasure chest of good memories and precious lessons. It's a nice place to visit, but I don't need to live there or it becomes a trap and a seedbed of regrets and longings that can't be quenched. The present is the only place to pitch my tent. It has all the people, issues, blessings, and opportunities I need. I hope to cherish each present moment for the remainder of my days.

Or, as the apostle Paul put it so much better, may I press on toward the goal that calls me heavenward (Philippians 3:14).

And finish the race well.

27

Gratitude

Where Was the Thank-You Note?

⊷

Gratitude is not only the greatest of virtues,
but the parent of all the others.
—Marcus Tullius Cicero

Years ago, we weathered a family crisis. This one fell short of the ultimate threat when Kris' life was later on the line with her cancer diagnosis. Still, it was a rough time, and our hearts were broken. The specifics are beside the point.

Kris and I were on our knees, praying through our tears and beseeching God to intervene, to fix the problem, and to set our world back on course.

Eventually, the storm passed and the sun shined upon us again. One year later, life had settled down again, though we carried the hurts in our memories. Kris turned to me one evening and said, "Ward, did you ever say thank you?"

"Thank you for what?"

"Did you ever say thank you to God for answering our prayer?"

I gave some thought to her question and realized two things: (1) Kris was right, and God had answered our prayer; and (2) it hadn't so much as occurred to me to say thank you. And why was that? I could only conclude that it was because God had taken too long to answer our prayers. That is, by the time the crisis was resolved, I'd forgotten about the way we'd prayed to God, pouring out our hearts, weeping, pleading with Him to hear us. When the situation was resolved, I simply took it in stride as the way of things, rather than a blessing from God in response to our supplications.

I came across the story recorded in Luke 17 that reflected this problem. Jesus came across a band of ten men with leprosy—a common thing in the ancient world. They were despised outcasts who clung together on the fringes of society. Jesus saw them, felt deep compassion, and healed all ten of them. But only one of them, we're told, came back to say thank you. He was identified as a Samaritan, someone accustomed to disrespect even without leprosy.

Jesus asked, "Were not all ten cleansed? Where are the other nine? Has no one returned to give praise to God except this foreigner?" (Luke 17:17–18)

Like Jesus, I'm appalled—until I consider my own record. How many blessings have I been given? How many answers to prayer? And how many times did I think to express my gratitude?

It's not that I haven't taken prayer seriously. I've always known prayer is a mystery and answered prayer is an even deeper one. At one time, I kept a prayer list of people and situations. I filed it away in my desk drawer and inevitably forgot all about it until, just as inevitably, the prayer list resurfaced. We were moving our offices, and I was cleaning out my desk. There it was; the prayer concerns of another era of my life.

I sat back and studied the names and the items, realizing each one was a matter of prayer I'd laid before God. Now, from the separation of time, it was possible to see the many strange and unpredictable ways God had addressed each issue on the list. In His own time and wisdom, He had been quietly and faithfully at work. What a mercy that He wasn't as forgetful as I was! Here was the prayer list, and there were His answers—and where was the thank-you note?

That unexpected faith exercise reinforced my belief that God hears and answers every single prayer. What isn't guaranteed, of course, is the nature of His answer. He responds in wisdom rather than subservience to our whims, and that's one more thing to be thankful for. I don't know where I'd be if He gave me everything I wanted when I wanted it, but it wouldn't be good. I realize that His ways are not my ways, and His wisdom is to be trusted. The Creator of the universe, I need to realize, has all the inside information—leave it all to Him.

Then I see that Paul has admonished us in the Scriptures to be thankful in all circumstances. Is that even remotely possible? In my younger foolishness, I might have said no. Farther down the trail, I'm beginning to change my answer. It's a matter of how much I trust God.

One afternoon, in the midst of an extremely jam-packed, stress-inducing day full of headaches and frustration, I gave myself a timeout. This was, of course, the strategy we'd use on our children to curb their poor behavior. I was tired, frustrated with myself and the world, and figuring I must be toxic to others. I retreated to the solace of my small office at home, closed the door, laid down on the sofa, and began a full-on, woe-is-me pity party. Fortunately, I came to my senses relatively quickly, stepping back to look at myself objectively and realize my problems amounted to a hill of beans. In short, I was whining—fully deserving of a child's punishment.

As better sense crashed my pity party, I asked myself whether I could really be thankful in such a situation, as Paul prescribes. Just a few minutes ago, I'd believed the weight of the world was on my shoulders. I was having a bad day—where did gratitude figure in?

"For one thing," said an almost imperceptible whisper in my soul, "you're breathing, right? For another, here you are sitting in a comfortable home, looking out a window with a spectacular view of the woods in the full glory of autumn."

Now I was listening.

The voice continued, "You have a wife you love, and she's alive and well and by your side every day. And here's another day when you haven't received a terrible call on the phone—say, giving news of some tragic automobile accident involving one of your children. And ..."

"That's enough," I said, slipping from the cushion of the chair and balancing on my knees on the floor, where I began talking to God. For once, I wasn't asking; I was *thanking*. And it was a tonic to my spirit. Why didn't I do this thanking thing more often?

What an amazing transformation just within a few minutes—from the classic wake-up-on-the-wrong-side-of-the-bed day full of misery to a wonderful day, an extraordinary day in which I was filled with realizations of blessings. A kind of Christmas morning of the spirit, unwrapping all the gifts of heaven. I knew that only God could have wrought such a change in the weather inside me so quickly—which was yet another gift from Him.

Certainly no antidepressant on the market would do this. I felt new energy. I felt the smile on my face, and I really believe I felt the smile on God's face as well. What was different? I was simply composing the thank-you note in my spirit, but I was also shifting a burden from my knobby shoulders to the infinitely wide and powerful shoulders of the Lord. By counting my blessings, I was also acknowledging His presence in my challenges.

I finally began to learn that gratitude trumps every other emotion. Indeed, Paul, who teaches us this, had one rotten day after another. He recounts a list of "distressings" rather than blessings, telling us he has been insulted, arrested, beaten, shipwrecked, stoned, impoverished, hungry, bleeding, imprisoned, and any number of other calamities (2 Corinthians 11:23–28). By choosing to be thankful in all circumstances, to rejoice in the Lord always, he made himself "bulletproof"; he declared himself, in advance, the winner of every future bout with misfortune, because God was with him. Nothing knocked him down yet, and nothing would.

Such an attitude is the gift that keeps giving. It causes you to have all kinds of good thoughts you wouldn't have enjoyed before, because you've untwisted your perspective; you're seeing life through 20/20 glasses. I realized with a bit of a start the other day that, at the moment, I had no major crises in my life. No urgent prayer requests. No concerns to make me toss and turn at night. Indeed, everything was terrific with my family and extended family. I saw the oncologist and everything is still indolent—my medical conditions are sluggish, and I can't help but wonder if an improved spirit has something to do with that.

One day, I was skiing the steep slopes in Telluride, surrounded by the spectacular beauties of jagged snow-covered peaks against brilliant cobalt skies. I was completely in the moment. It was a good moment—one of those you wish you could put in a jar and preserve, although who knows? The following moment might be even better.

But how could it? I told Kris that I didn't consider it likely that life would ever again be as good as it is in the present. When things are going well, my worries and irritations are indolent. They just can't get any traction, and they slip to some smaller level where I'm much less conscious of them. Gratitude and thanksgiving keep them at bay. They're the light that drives away the darkness.

Can happiness really be this simple? Can we just put on our "thank-you hats" and ride into the sunset? Of course not. We're created to experience intense joy, but we couldn't even appreciate that joy if we didn't also have our portion of sorrow. A considerable element of the contentment Kris and I feel is the product of having walked together through the valley of the shadow of death during her bout with cancer. The pain of that time makes the joy of this time so much more palpable. Gratitude, I feel, is the element that gives us the high ground so that we can see the whole landscape—the highs and lows, the mountains and valleys. What we're left with then is the goodness and faithfulness of God and the hope of what lies ahead with Him. And out of this perspective comes peace and contentment.

My mentor, Monty Sholund, began each day the same way he'd end it: on his knees. In the morning, he'd offer a prayer for a fresh anointing of God's Spirit. In the evening, he'd express his gratitude and this thought: "Lord, I hope you found me pleasing today."

Me too.

Part of that perspective is understanding who's who. I'm a knucklehead, and God is the Creator of the universe. I am the child, and He is the Father. He answers my prayers, but in His time, in His wisdom, and in His way. Once my mind is settled on that, I'm capable of feeling the gratitude I need to express.

Thank you.

Acknowledgments

Many people contributed to making *Bigger Than Me* possible, and I am most grateful for their help and support:

My family—Kris, Andy, Sarah, and Mike, and my mom—for patiently putting up with me for so many years. Each of you has been a gift from God.

Rick Warren, for all his wisdom and encouragement in addition to his gift of writing the foreword.

Presidents George W. Bush and Barack Obama for providing me with an opportunity to serve both Africa and my country.

Jay Bennett and Mark Sweeney, who have been partners with me in every aspect of *Bigger Than Me* from the very beginning.

Lynn Voelbel, Heidi Morgan, Robb Suggs, and Bill Watkins whose brilliant editing helped frame the manuscript, and Rich Voelbel, who holds me accountable in life.

The many friends who believed in this book and were of great encouragement, including Sarah Groves, Rich Stearns, Cris Carter, Paul Bennett, Marilyn Nelson-Carlson, Kathleen Blatz, Arthur Rouner, Greg Page, Paul Bennett, Joe Ritchie, Jack Leslie, Raj Shah, Mike Sime, Keith Moyer, Steve Brehm, Sen. Dave Durenberger, Judge Paul Magnuson, Arthur Rouner, Lori Olsen, Mark Thompson, Atul Tandon, Joseph Voelbel, Steve Moore, Jeff Bird, Whitney MacMillan, Larry Rybka, Daniel Wordsworth, Peb Jackson, BJ Goergen, Ralph Veerman, Larry Julian, Dr. Greg Vercillotii, Mark Thompson, Rev. John Ross, John Busacker, Larry Julian, Phil Styrlund, Eric Fellman, and Widdy Bird.

Thanks to the entire Tuesday Prayer Group that has been meeting for nineteen years and provides accountability, prayer, insight into Scripture, and deep friendship.

Also with great respect and admiration to my friends in

Washington, DC, who faithfully follow Jesus, despite living in the cyclotron of politics, including US Senators Jim Inhofe, Chris Coons, Mike Enzi, John Boozman, John Hoeven, Amy Klobuchar, John Barrasso, and Representatives Erik Paulsen, Betty McCollum, and Tom Emmer. Also heartfelt thanks to Mark Powers, Luke Holland, Ed Meese, Elizabeth Dias, Amb. Stuart Symington, Mark Brinkmoeller, Amb. Mark Green, Gov. David Beasley, Amb. Tony Hall, and Amb. Linda Thomas Greenfield.

And special thanks for support from the entire "family of friends" in the International Fellowship convening small groups all around the world.

Thanks to Carlton Garborg, David Sluka, and the entire team at BroadStreet Publishing who took a chance on this book and have been so very helpful.

And in memory of my dad, who was taken far too early. I miss him every day.

Notes

Chapter 3

1 Rodney M. Howard-Browne, *Seeing Jesus as He Really Is* (Nashville, TN: World Publishing, 1999), n.p.
2 Dorothy L. Sayers, *Creed or Chaos* (New York: Harcourt Brace, 1949), 56.

Chapter 4

1 Jonathan Swift, *Thoughts on Various Subjects* (1711), n.p.

Chapter 5

1 Ward Brehm, "Alone but Not Alone" (unpublished poem written at Pacem in Terris hermitage, November 2012).

Chapter 6

1 http://www.worldprayers.org/archive/prayers/invocations/may_god_bless_you_with_a_restless.html.

Chapter 7

1 Richard A. Swenson, *A Minute of Margin: Restoring Balance to Busy Lives—180 Daily Reflections*, Pilgrimage Growth Guide series (Colorado Springs: Nav Press, 2003), n.p.

Chapter 8

1 Ward Brehm, "Masquerade" (unpublished poem written at Pacem in Terris hermitage sanctuary, August 16, 2016).
2 Richard Rohr, meditation entitled "Aweism," adapted from "Nature and the Soul," *Radical Grace* 24:3 (Summer 2011), 3, 22; Richard Rohr, *In the Footsteps of Francis: Awakening to Creation*, January 19, 2015, https://cac.org/.
3 Oswald Chambers, *My Utmost for His Highest* (Grand Rapids, MI: Discovery House, 1935), January 31.
4 Ibid.

Chapter 12

1 *Wall Street*, directed by Oliver Stone (1987; Los Angeles: 20th Century Fox, 2010), DVD.

2   *MSN Money*; Randy Alcorn, *Money, Possessions, and Eternity*, rev. ed. (Carol Stream, IL: Tyndale House, 2003), 291; Richard Stearns, *The Hole in Our Gospel* (Nashville, TN: W Publishing, 2010), 216.

Chapter 14

1   Richard Rohr, *Breathing Under Water: Spirituality and the Twelve Steps* (Cincinnati, OH: Franciscan Media, 2011), 8–9.
2   Ibid.
3   Elton Trueblood, quoted in Bill Hull, *Choose the Life: Exploring a Faith that Embraces Discipleship* (Grand Rapids, MI: Baker, 2004), 214–215.

Chapter 22

1   Vance Havner, Goodreads, http://www.goodreads.com/quotes/97169 -god-uses-broken-things-it-takes-broken-soil-to-produce.
2   Billy Graham, "Blessed by Burdens," *Unto the Hills: A Daily Devotional* (Nashville, TN: Thomas Nelson, 2010), March 31.

Chapter 24

1   Ward Brehm, "The Good Wife" (unpublished poem written at Pacem in Terris hermitage, October 2014).

About the Author

Ward Brehm is a Twin Cities businessman, a leader in African humanitarian efforts, and a nationally known public speaker and commentator on relief and development in Africa.

In 2004 President Bush appointed Brehm to be chairman of the United States African Development Foundation (USADF), following confirmation by the US Senate, where he served until 2009. In 2010 President Obama reappointed Brehm to the board of the USADF, where he continues to serve.

He also is a member of the Council of Foreign Relations, and he currently serves on the board of directors of the American Refugee Committee (ARC) based in Minneapolis. At ARC, he helped found the Asili initiative, which brings a network of proven social businesses together into an enterprise platform that delivers essential services—clean water, quality health care, and agricultural livelihoods—at affordable prices to Eastern Congo, using a locally owned for profit business platform.

In 2008, Brehm brought his message as an advocate for the poor in Africa to the National Prayer Breakfast, where he gave the keynote address before an audience including the US President, First Lady, foreign heads of state, most members of Congress, and the Washington diplomatic community. Brehm was the first person from the US business community to be asked by Congress to address this annual gathering in Washington, DC.

Brehm was awarded the Presidential Citizenship Medal—the country's second-highest civilian honor—for his work in Africa at an Oval Office ceremony with President George W. Bush and First Lady Laura Bush in December of 2008.

In addition to *Bigger Than Me*, Brehm is also the author of two books on his experiences in Africa, *Life Through A Different Lens* and *White Man Walking*.

Brehm recently sold the insurance consulting companies he founded, and now engages in full-time humanitarian work in Africa as an unofficial ambassador for Jesus. He and his wife, Kris, live and work in Minneapolis, MN.

Backstage with Bono, talking about Africa

*Receiving the Presidential Citizenship Medal in
the Oval Office with President George W. Bush*

*Keynote at the National Prayer Breakfast
in Washington, DC*

BiggerThanMeBook.com